Power and Punishment
in Scott's Novels

Power and Punishment

IN

Scott's Novels

Bruce Beiderwell

The University of Georgia Press
Athens and London

© 1992 by the University of Georgia Press
Athens, Georgia 30602
All rights reserved
Designed by Debby Jay
Set in Linotron Century Expanded
The paper in this book meets the guidelines
for permanence and durability of the Committee on
Production Guidelines for Book Longevity
of the Council on Library Resources.

Printed in the United States of America

96   95   94   93   92   C   5   4   3   2   1

Library of Congress Cataloging in Publication Data

Beiderwell, Bruce John.
Power and punishment in Scott's novels / Bruce Beiderwell.
p.   cm.
Includes bibliographical references (p.   ) and index.
ISBN 0-8203-1351-3 (alk. paper)
1. Scott, Walter, Sir, 1771–1832—Political and social views.
2. Power (Social sciences) in literature.
3. Punishment in literature.
4. Crime in literature.
I. Title.
PR5343.P68B45   1992
823'.7—dc20   90-23277
CIP

British Library Cataloging in Publication Data available

Contents

Preface

This book will argue that Walter Scott's literary career was part of (not merely paralleled by) an active and vital period in the history of criminal law reform. That history continues to weigh upon us today in our own confusion concerning the state's right to punish and its purpose in punishing. The political climate of the nineteenth century's early decades powerfully anticipates that of more recent history. Thinking is still bound by the methods and motives apparent nearly two centuries ago in Bentham's "censorial" or critical analysis of the law, in parliamentary efforts to focus and thereby effectuate the threat of capital punishment, and in strenuous attempts to protect the law's sophisticated machinery against such reform efforts.

Scott helps us understand matters of punishment and power (in both his time and ours) because he uneasily straddled the conflicting and complicated interests evident in an age of transition. Indeed his novels both comment upon and represent what Foucault has identified as the shift from the body to the "soul" of the criminal in the exercise of punishment—that is, the shift *from* thinking of punishment as the infliction of pain *to* thinking of punishment as part of an elaborate administrative machinery of control. But what we term a transition surely seemed for Scott a crisis. What many historians now see as a conspiracy of power he more likely saw as a necessary though uncertain response to chaotic, threatening forces of change. We should note that punishments in Scott's time were intended to address immediate social problems, not so much to realize justice or to achieve grandly conceived social ideals; such goals were reserved for philosophers and philanthropists. Yet Scott commands our interest not for his deference to things as they were—rather, for the scope of his vision. The Waverley novels make it clear that Scott maintained his conservatism with an unsettling, complex appreciation of the moral and political limitations of existings laws; he felt himself more a beleaguered figure than a privileged one.

The moral challenges that Scott faced in his novels were of his making—that is to say, a result of his own understanding of the human complexity underlying social and political phenomena. He raises in his fictions problematic issues of justice and power, of right and efficiency. And scenes of punishment in the Waverley novels display the especially fine tension that power must sustain in its active operation. Particularly in his early novels, Scott tests the rightness or goodness of the power he upholds against its most unpleasant expression: he follows the state's claim to authority over the individual to its discomforting conclusion in an act of legal killing. But as we shall see, Scott also finds ways to circumvent (through his authority as novelist) the implicit challenges posed to political authority by its own most severe actions.

Clearly the manner of punishment, as well as the basis upon which the state claims its right to punish, bears upon the subject of power. And however precarious or compromised he imagined that power to be, Scott—as an author and citizen—was on its side. This conservative quality makes Scott an especially instructive figure: he cannot—like the radical Godwin—simply use the unpleasantness of punishment to enlist the sympathies of readers on behalf of the punished; he must defend, overcome, explain, or explain away that very unpleasantness. Scenes of punishment in the Waverley novels manifest Scott's difficult position of authority both as a political being and a novelist in regard to various problematic questions: Is the purpose of punishment deterrence or retribution? On what grounds does the state claim the power to punish? In terms of Scott's sense of history, can punishment be understood as a measure of civilization? Scott's novels present no systematic or consistent response to such questions, but even their inconsistencies tell us much: the Waverley novels clarify the burdensome responsibility involved in the act of punishment and the consequent attractiveness of escaping that responsibility.

One can best appreciate Scott's political anxieties in the early Waverley novels, for these works most openly expose the exercise of power in acts of punishment and wrestle with the effects of these acts. *Waverley* suggests the contrary and unwelcome effects of excessive severity. *Old Mortality* assesses punishment as a symbolic claim to (and representation of) legitimate power. *Rob Roy* juxtaposes radically separate civil orders and in doing so uncovers the moral relationship of those who materially benefit from punishment to those who punish. And *The Heart of Midlothian* traces the ambiguities of history and judgment that frustrate the pursuit of justice. In these works, Scott displays an insightful detachment that we may underestimate or even deny in our attention to the cultural context that surrounds, defines, and shapes the productions of an author.

But throughout Scott's career there operates an opposing impulse that we are perhaps more sensitive to—a profound desire to make fiction correspond to wishes. Novelistic punishments can, after all, realize justice or project a sense of power operating disinterestedly in pursuit of justice more easily than can actual punishments. A fictional hanging in 1814 could take place (and generally did) in the gaps of a narrative, where morally distracting specifics of the victim's ordeal remain unspoken; but a real hanging in the same year would be a public event. It is both striking and instructive to note that the disgust Quentin Durward (one of Scott's more forceful medieval heroes) feels at the practice of leaving an offender's corpse to rot in the sun does not necessarily reflect a modern, imagined response to an ancient custom. In August 1832, one month before Scott's death, the corpse of a criminal who had been publicly hanged was by order of law left hanging in chains— exposed to the elements and to public observation. Thirty thousand people witnessed the hanging; many thousands of others viewed the body in the ensuing weeks. This was the last officially sanctioned display of the victim's body in Great Britain, although the practice of public executions continued until 1868. In editing out or eliding the open brutality of such a policy, Scott seeks to construct fictions of more subtle and satisfying power—fictions that effectively undergird power by dissolving the tensions created by its active and public exercise.

These inherently conservative projections of wishful ideals are most apparent in Scott's later works. The exotic medieval romances, for example, make justice the inevitable product of the physical acts of just men: victory defines virtue. And in the case of *Redgauntlet*, a last variation on the Jacobite theme, victory (and with it justice) precedes the narrative and makes the state's action unnecessary. This story of the late eighteenth century posits an established government that simply cannot be challenged: the

rightness of the Hanoverian order makes the order itself unassailable. In such romances of justice and power the vexing problems of
punishment are dissolved rather than resolved, and the means of
this dissolution tell us much: perhaps the problems of punishment
are so tenacious and varied because they grow from irreconcilable
notions and feelings; revenge, retribution, utility, sympathy, forgiveness—these words suggest a range of emotional possibilities,
of human desires or goals, that surround the pursuit of justice.

The late works diminish the complexities of the earlier novels
in ways that mirror recurrent and familiar debates. In *Redgauntlet* and "The Two Drovers," for example, the growing impulse for
privacy, for "kindness," indeed for the modern system of imprisonment and execution becomes more apparent. Yet the violence in
some of Scott's medieval novels suggests an ambivalence deeply
rooted in legal history: a modern system of imprisonment (and its
myth of correction or reformation) seems unsatisfying when placed
against the closure promised by the punishment of death. In the
Waverley novels—as in our own unresolved attitudes toward imprisonment and execution—we can see that conflicting myths of
justice and power possess their own substantial reality. It seems
that novels anticipate and shape history: they do not merely reflect
events, but are part of what we apprehend as historical reality.

With this relationship in mind, we need not look only to Great
Britain in the age of reform to discover meaningful connections
made between fictions and civil policy. We may engage our own
critical faculties and note that the perceived failure of the prison
is now (in the United States at least) turning attention back to
the body of the criminal. It remains to be seen if, for example,
the current rhetoric and behavior of state courts, legislators, and
governors regarding capital punishment indicates a general trend
toward severity or is merely a temporary aberration. But contemporary popular fiction and (more important) the use we find
for fiction suggests a turn away from the abolitionist spirit of
the Supreme Court's ruling on the *Furman* v. *Georgia* case and
toward seemingly decisive, physical displays of justice and power.
Frustrated by the inadequacies of the penitentiary (a place of spiritual renewal) or the correctional institute (a secular or therapeutic
equivalent), some find the formula of death attractively reductive.

In *For Capital Punishment*, Walter Berns (an author of numerous books on constitutional law) uses his reading experience

of *Macbeth* and Camus's *L'Etranger* to express an intuitive sense of justice that depends upon the ultimate punishment. Berns asks which fiction—Shakespeare's or Camus's—most fully meets a reader's sense of the real world? *Macbeth* embodies a vision in which the physical expression of popular anger is a consequence of individual villainy. *L'Etranger* makes anger a fraudulent expression of a convention-bound society that values neither people nor ideas enough to generate deeply felt, retributive action.

Berns's comparison works upon an apt yet unacknowledged irony (one that Scott, the inveterate problematizer of history and fiction, would be wary of): Berns asks his readers to refer to imaginary works of literature to better analyze and construct the world they actually inhabit. The force of this argument as well as its uncertain morality becomes more clear as Berns shifts from the comparison between *Macbeth* and *L'Etranger* to the constructions of contemporary culture: the liberal contractual theories of the Enlightenment reformer Cesare Beccaria lead on until "the insurance policy takes the place of law enforcement and the posse comitatus, and John Wayne and Gary Cooper, give way to Mutual of Omaha."

By such means, Berns obliterates distinctions between law enforcement and capital punishment and further reduces the necessary complexity of the state's exercise of the death penalty to the structural and moral clarity of a conventional Western film. It is as if Scott were to argue in, say, the *Quarterly Review* that judicial combat as presented in *Ivanhoe* is in fact the best means to circumvent the tangles of the modern trial because the combat in *Ivanhoe* always achieves an unambiguous justice. Scott had, in fact, noted that judicial combat must have been a thoroughly haphazard means to justice; unlike Berns, he seems quite capable of separating himself from (as well as indulging in) the illusory moral closure fiction makes available. To be fair, Berns's argument does not depend wholly upon his uncritical appropriation of popular mythology: but his use of popular figures to validate an argument for capital punishment suggests how powerfully those figures may operate in shaping one's civil imagination.

Elements of what Walter Bagehot referred to as the "boyish fancy" of battle in *Ivanhoe* are in many respects at the root of what Berns admires in Westerns. In both prevails an implicit faith that good eventually will physically triumph in what Bagehot calls "fighting time." Yet the critical impulse apparent in Scott's

scenes of execution in a novel like *The Heart of Midlothian* helps
point to another irony left hanging in Berns's discussion. Although
Berns is right to characterize Mersault's execution as unsatisfying, we must remember that Mersault is executed by law whereas
Macbeth is destroyed in battle. Berns remarks on the dramatic
appropriateness of the final showdown between Macbeth and Mac-
duff, but in doing so he loses the connection he had posited between
art and law.

Scott shrewdly appreciates the dramatic significance of the connection sustained and broken in such analogies. He often makes
it plain that the fiction of law in a modern, civil society responds
to, reflects, and generates a morally and functionally complex network of human relations. Yet he too feels the uneasiness that arises
between the law's intricate operation and what we desire—simple
justice. And he too is capable of resolving that uneasiness with
simple fictions. The Waverley novels explore notions of punishment and power that are sustained not only by our understanding
but by our dreams.

Acknowledgments

I've received good advice and much appreciated encouragement on this project. Frederick Burwick, Daniel Cottom, Jean Hampton, Suzy Holstein, Joseph Janangelo, Maximillian Novak, Judith Wilt, and Stephen Yeazell read and sensitively responded to all or parts of the manuscript at various stages of its development. Others have provided less direct—but no less real or valuable—assistance: Charles L. Batten, Patrick Ford, and Farrell Webb. Thanks are also due to *Clio*, *Philological Quarterly*, and *Studies in Romanticism* for permission to reprint portions of this book that first appeared in their pages. Nancy Atkinson gave the manuscript a meticulous final reading. And Nancy Grayson Holmes, of the University of Georgia Press, has been an attentive and supportive editor. I am especially grateful to Bruce Richardson, whose wide learning, wit, and friendship were steadily evident to me in his conversation about things related and unrelated to Scott; to Shari Zimmerman, whose help seemed to take the right form at the right time unerringly; and to Alexander Welsh, whose insights on matters of law and literature were provocative—even inspiring. To all of my readers I apologize for any mistakes that remain in this book by saying—with Sam Weller—"It's over, and can't be helped, and that's one consolation, as they always says in Turkey, ven they cuts the wrong man's head off."

In assorted ways I also want to thank those who I trust will forgive me when I do indeed cut the wrong man's head off: Karin Baloian, Don Beiderwell, Renata Gusmão-Garcia. My mother, Helen Beiderwell, deserves special thanks. And also do my father, Therman, and brother Steve—both of whom I will remember. My son, Samuel, will need more years of schooling before he can read this book, but when he can—and when he gets to this page—I want him to know how much I've learned from him, and how deeply I've appreciated the lessons. Finally, my love and gratitude to Ivna Gusmão, who says, *"quem te viu, quem te ve!"* Her vision has proven irresistible.

Power and Punishment
in Scott's Novels

Introduction

————··⟨∞⟩··————

ONE of the pamphlets in Walter Scott's huge, thirteen-volume edition of Lord Somers's tracts—a collection of political writings from the late seventeenth and early eighteenth centuries—concerns the stabbing of an adviser to King William by a desperate French agent, Antoine de Guiscard. The Duke of Ormand, who helped subdue Guiscard after the attack, must answer a strikingly direct question posed by the would-be assassin: "My Lord Ormand, pour quoy ne may depeches vous; 'Why don't you dispatch me?'" The duke's "memorable answer" acknowledges the inevitability of Guiscard's punishment while it shifts that unpleasant responsibility onto an unspecified and somehow less fastidious actor: "Ce n'est pas l'affair des honestes gens; C'est l'affair d'une autre ('Tis not the work of gentlemen, 'tis the work of others)."[1] By this shift the duke puts an imaginary moral distance between the act of punishment and the power that authorizes it.

Apparent in Ormand's answer to Guiscard is a confusion regarding the right and propriety of "dispatching" the criminal. Considered in this context, his answer is surely more "memorable" than adequate. The duke may assume that as a member of a civilized society he has surrendered the right to punish. But his exclusion of "honestes gens" from the act of punishment muddles the moral responsibility or meaning of his surrender. After all, who benefits from the exercise of punishment if not honest gentlemen? Ormand refuses to acknowledge the disturbing idea that the foundation of the state's right to punish consists partly in his own surrender to the state. Furthermore, he undercuts that foundation by suggesting that the hangman's lowness is inseparable from the repulsiveness of his commission. Essentially the duke implies that the deed of justice—the actual act of execution—has no connection to the deliberation of justice that led to it. He assumes the executioner must be bad enough for the task at hand; a more rigorous examination of his own responsibility would make him insist (at least in theory) that the executioner be good enough to carry out the role entrusted to him.

Like Ormand, Quentin Durward (one of Scott's more active fictional heroes) resists implicating himself—or those higher than himself—in an act of punishment: he hedges at enlisting in the Scottish Guard of Louis XI because the bodies of criminals are left hanging too near the castle of the king (*Quentin Durward*, chap. 3, pp. 23–24).[2] Quentin soon learns that the closeness of Louis's castle to the hanging tree signals an inescapable relationship: the right to punish must be located somewhere, and preferably not in the executioner himself. Neither Ormand nor Quentin intends to grant the hangman such authority, but their modest attempts to disassociate the power that orders an execution from the functionary that performs it reveal a troubling uncertainty concerning various moral and practical matters raised in the act of punishment. Dickens's crazed hangman Dennis, from his historical novel *Barnaby Rudge* (a kind of homage to Scott), clarifies this muddle by dramatically exaggerating the mistakenly radical split between power and performer. Dennis considers opportunities to kill as his right—a right that the state too often interferes with. Detached from those who bestow his power upon him, Dennis becomes a comic nightmare that concretely represents the ends of political irresponsibility.

But in addition to the considerations of right and propriety evident in Dennis's zeal for violence or in Ormand's answer to Guiscard, Quentin's response to an accomplished fact of a hanging invites attention to important questions of policy. Quentin's instinctive humanity checks his trust in a monarch who seems oblivious to the sight and stench of a body left dangling from a tree.[3] In one instance, Quentin vigorously albeit unwittingly challenges the king's right to punish when he cuts down a criminal suffering the agonies of death. As a newcomer to France, the Scottish knight does not appreciate the import of the fleur-de-lis scratched into the hanging tree, but from the dangerous consequences of his ignorance he learns to maintain a shrewdly self-protective and critical attitude toward Louis's authority. And if his repudiation of Louis becomes ever more discreet as the novel progresses, it also becomes more self-conscious and determined. In response to the cruel and arbitrary punishments that Louis sanctions, Quentin devotes to the king only a fraction of the loyalty he is capable of sustaining. Of course, Scott presents Louis XI as a "sagacious and most politic monarch" who well understands the limits of the loyalty he inspires, or rather extorts, through fear—chiefly through the threat of punishment. But Quentin responds easily and faithfully to honorable appeals; he accepts a commission under Louis only because he has no alternative and always seeks to limit or escape that commission.

Such complex and often discomforting issues of right, justice, and power that surround an act of punishment recur throughout Scott's fiction. We should not be surprised at this fact. Scott was, after all, educated to practice law—not to write novels. Furthermore, his interest in history generally focused on times of rebellion or revolution—times that brought into question the state's authority to make laws and the people's right to challenge them. Finally, Scott was an embattled Tory in an age of reform—and much reforming zeal in the eighteenth and early nineteenth centuries was expended specifically on the problem of how to punish wrongdoers. As recent critics have striven to appreciate the political dimensions of the works of romantic writers, there has been a growing (although belated) recognition of Scott's significant place in literary and social history.[4] Scott should continue to profit from the reconceiving of romanticism, from a criticism that no longer strives to separate the individual writer's genius or "imagination" from the broader culture.[5] But I believe also that Scott's importance (so widely recognized by his contemporaries) extends to our present imperfect understanding of the problems of punishment and their relationship to power, for his indecisive and shifting responses to these problems strike me as immediate and familiar in reference to our own uncertainties.

We may identify in the Waverley novels two distinct modes of response to the issues raised by punishment that point to Scott's peculiar modernity: at times, Scott addresses the issues; at other times, he dissolves them. To be more specific, in *Waverley* (1814) Scott feels a personal, moral responsibility in subscribing to the state's right to punish; therefore, he attempts to justify or (failing to justify) to criticize the execution of Fergus Mac-Ivor. Yet in

Ivanhoe (1820) Scott gives voice to a comforting fiction of justice
that equates punishment with guilt; injustice in this later work
simply cannot take full shape in an act of punishment. These opposing modes of response to vexing, concrete problems parallel
the distinction between the novel and the romance as they were
understood by Scott and his contemporaries: the novel was supposed to submit to the experience of real life, whereas the romance
was allowed to indulge in a strong element of fantasy.[6] The Waverley novels encompass this distinction; the specific moral, political,
and historical conditions that dominate Scott's early novels of the
recent past are imaginatively transcended in some of his later
works. In the exotic romances of medieval times—*Ivanhoe* and
The Talisman—and in that curiously revised return to Jacobite
themes—*Redgauntlet*—Scott substitutes wishful and manageable
visions for the realistic and vexing difficulties that generally apply
in *Waverley, Old Mortality, Rob Roy,* and *The Heart of Midlothian.*

It is unnecessary to announce that there are bad Waverley
novels, and that most of the worst of these novels belong to the
later part of Scott's extraordinarily productive career. It should
be clear at the outset, however, that I do not separate early novels
from late romances in order to exalt one group over the other. By
such means many critics have attempted to rescue a few of Scott's
works from the general neglect they all share. The invidious tendencies of these efforts may be illustrated by the common mistake
of limiting the use of the term "Waverley novels" to the novels of
Scotland's history. The term, of course, was used to designate all
fiction by the anonymous "Author of *Waverley.*" The Scott canon
remains mixed and unwieldy despite efforts to clarify or shrink
it by definitions of genre or subject. Recent books by Jane Millgate and Judith Wilt argue that the Waverley novels possess a
collective identity.[7] We may, then, better understand individual
works by keeping alert to the context established by the series.
We may be prepared to appreciate certain features of the late
romances by reading them as significant variations on (or developments of) a single, complex theme established in the earlier novels.
The distinction I make between "novel" and "romance," therefore,
concerns Scott's treatment of theme; it follows Scott's own conventional understanding of genre and serves to identify and underscore the opposing critical and wishful tendencies of his fictions—

tendencies that are apparent from the start of his career but are more clearly marked in view of his whole career. Scott's shifting aesthetic response to the profound responsibility inherent in the act of punishment offers us a lesson in the ethics of fiction.

In his early novels of postrevolutionary Great Britain, Scott addresses the problem of punishment with some courage and much insight. Scenes of punishment in these novels draw our attention to the moral and practical difficulties power assumes when it asserts itself over an individual's right to life. Scott's attempts to justify the fictional executions he presents may be likened to the lawmaker's efforts regarding punishment, for Scott's support (both in novels and in life) of the order established by the revolution of 1688 places him in the same uncomfortable position of responsibility that a lawmaker must endure; Scott sides with authority in a way different from that of most novelists who preceded him.[8] The result is that the death penalty in, for example, *Waverley* severely tests Scott's assurance in the legitimacy or at least the extent of Hanoverian authority. Even one so assured of the law's excellence as William Blackstone feels the same test: "To shed the blood of our fellow-creature is a matter that requires the greatest deliberation and the fullest conviction of our own authority."[9] But Blackstone's *Commentaries* exude greater satisfaction in that authority than do Scott's early novels, which present and analyze scenes of punishment in complex ways. In Scott's realistic works, great deliberation is more apparent than full conviction.

Perhaps Scott's reluctance to accept the responsibility of his authority as novelist can be linked to his sense of uneasiness regarding the messages conveyed by scenes of punishment. Scott had achieved distinction as an editor with the publication of the *Minstrelsy of the Scottish Border* in 1802, and fame as a poet with the publication of *The Lay of the Last Minstrel* in 1805; but his name lent no credit to the products of the last phase of his literary career, which commenced with the publication of *Waverley*. Although Scott could not keep readers from identifying him as "The Great Unknown," he stubbornly maintained an official anonymity concerning the novels until after his financial ruin in 1826. Furthermore, the various authorial filters employed most elaborately in the Waverley novels published before *Ivanhoe* (invented editors, storytellers, antiquarians, and schoolteachers) manifestly complicate the relationship of Scott to the historical matter of his fiction. The shifting narrative perspectives, the editorial glosses, and the invocation of historical distance in the early novels of the recent past make it difficult to pin down Scott's position on the justice and utility of the executions he stages. But attempting to *pin down* Scott's position amongst these covers would miss the important point: it is the complex and even contradictory nature of the material—or Scott's willingness to allow for complexity and contradictions—that reward study. In short, the Author of *Waverley* is more intelligent than confident in his depiction of executions and the issues that invariably belong to executions.

No doubt it is easier to hang a person in fiction than in fact, yet profound questions concerning punishment come into play in novels. Scott's imagination registers a disturbing likeness that fictional executions have to real ones; he is sensitive to the justice or injustice, effectiveness or ineffectiveness of the punishments the law exacts in his novels. But Scott never completely forgets that his works are only stories; he maintains a distance—however unsteadily—toward his own creations. The distance as well as the discomfort is important. On the one hand, Scott (as a self-conscious writer of fictions) was free to explore the meaning and validity of different justifications of punishment; on the other hand, he was encouraged—almost forced—to make that effort by the closeness of the issues he raised to the world he inhabited. In the first four chapters I take up the novels that are generally marked by this critical perspective on punishment.

Waverley sets in motion a series of responses to multiple issues raised in an act of punishment. In this first novel, Scott implicitly endorses a common utilitarian justification of punishment only to find that justification wanting. The dramatically moving representation of Fergus Mac-Ivor's last days undermines the settled assurance expressed by the worthy Colonel Talbot concerning the justice and necessity of the execution. The hero's easy reconciliation of his own past and future history to Talbot's reasoning has long been the source of criticism leveled at both character and author. One might say that Scott was embarrassed by the realistic power of his own fiction. It seems highly unlikely that he fully anticipated the sympathies inspired by the trial and execution of Fergus and his follower Evan Dhu; certainly he had no master plan for the novel, but had followed the logic of the situation he had created.[10] In this respect, the writing of *Waverley* may be seen as a means of discovery for its author—even if that discovery proved unwelcome. It is just this imaginative, *a posteriori* process that makes Edwin Eigner classify Scott as a realist in opposition to those romance writers who refuse to be dominated by the causal logic of their own fiction.[11]

Waverley remains one of Scott's best novels, but he was not to reject the lesson it offered him in respect to its most notable awkwardness. In *Old Mortality*, *Rob Roy*, and *The Heart of Midlothian*, Scott cultivated an almost experimental and ultimately critical attitude toward the issues raised by scenes of punishment. Even the fanatical Burley of *Old Mortality*, for example, is allowed a fairly respectable position in his argument with the hero, Henry Morton, over the right invoked by the rebels in the killing of Archbishop Sharpe. After all, set against the brutality of the rebels is the equal brutality of the royalists. In *Rob Roy*, Scott registers a complex and highly personal response to the effectiveness of civilized law through the first-person narration of a proper hero who is simultaneously enriched and distressed by swift acts of primitive revenge. These considerations of utility, right, and revenge are gathered in what is perhaps Scott's most ambitious novel, *The Heart of Midlothian*. In that work, the Duke of Argyle offers a partial synthesis of competing responses to the problems of punishment. But Argyle's wisdom is not sufficient to solve—or make uninteresting—those problems. Taken as a whole, Scott's early novels provide an unsystematic and tentative yet perceptive and wide-ranging commentary on a subject of enduring importance.

The moral tension inherent in the act of punishment is generally accommodated by a significantly different kind of expression in Scott's later fiction. In *Ivanhoe*, *The Talisman*, and *Redgauntlet* Scott more eagerly translates discomfort into desire. In other words, the critical tendencies of realism are dispelled by the powerful wishes that shape romance.[12] All the virtuous Saxons in *Ivanhoe* act with an extraordinary assurance that justice cannot be defeated. A battle, therefore, becomes a trial, and the results of battle suffice as the punishment of wrongdoers. In *The Talisman* a similar confidence is apparent when the noble Saladin lops off the head of a murderer with godlike decisiveness: "the sabre of Saladin left its sheath as lightning leaves the cloud" (chap. 28, p. 310). No comparably grand images authorize the executions presented in the more realistic novels; those acts are more likely to be the type imagined by Ormand or observed by Quentin. We need only think of Porteous's unnecessary cruelty toward the condemned Wilson or the Doomster's primitive acts of torture in *Old Mortality* to note the difference between novelistic scenes of punishment, which grapple with human responses to pain, and romances, which deftly uncomplicate such responses.

Although *Redgauntlet* is usually considered Scott's last great Scottish novel—a triumphant return from the "tushery" of the medieval works—it, like the exotic romances, makes wishes prevail over realistic matters concerning an established power's exercise of punishment. In *Redgauntlet*, the cool and gentlemanly person of General Campbell, who casually dismisses a late and feeble Jacobite conspiracy, commands—like Saladin—an almost untouchable and virtuous power. But Campbell's power has little need to assert itself. Significantly, it belongs to a Great Britain not far removed in time from Scott's own day. Campbell's position toward the unregenerate Jacobites may be usefully compared to Ormand's toward Guiscard. The rebels of the novel and the French assassin of the historical incident both await their doom at the hands of a feared enemy. But the conditions of Scott's romance of power allow the general to take the edge off the question "Why don't you dispatch me?" For, unlike Ormand, Campbell can answer, in effect, "Because you are most effectively punished by my withholding punishment." Campbell does not need to punish the Jacobites in order to realize justice or to protect the established order. Since the rebels can do no harm to an order so secure, they may best be punished by the polite scorn of the government.

The wishful element in this scene is clarified if we compare it to a similar action that closes one of Scott's lesser-known novels. In *Peveril of the Peak*, the practical advantages of an act of royal grace are made explicit; Charles II overlooks Buckingham's treason because given the duke's reputation as a "zealous Protestant" it would be dangerous not to. But in a show of power held in reserve, the king makes it clear to Buckingham that he knows the precise extent of the aborted conspiracy. This knowledge and its potential use against Buckingham provides the background needed to appreciate the king's "kindness." Charles's political dexterity—not his forgiving nature—ends Buckingham's plot without, as the king says, "either hanging or marriage."[13] Of course, Charles is wrong in regard to the latter—there will be the obligatory joining of the proper hero and heroine, but he does get away without sanctioning legal ceremonies more discomforting (if no less final) than novelistic marriages (chap. 48, pp. 561–65).

Scott's shift from strenuous gropings after justice to dreams of justice, or from an analysis of power's source or legitimacy to a dream of power, suggests a pattern of thinking that reveals much about the crucial efforts of his age to direct the administration of the state's responsibility to punish. The consequences of these efforts remain with us today in our anxious attempts to find the most humane and discreet means of execution, and in our apparently fixed but ever-failing commitment to the prison as a correctional institution. Whatever the conscious intentions of the reformers of Scott's time, their chief accomplishment was to revise the shape and scope of the expression of power—not to shift the center of power. We should remember that significant reform of the criminal law in Great Britain awaited Peel's conservative administration.[14] As Michel Foucault has shown, punishment functions to communicate and fix relationships between state and citizen. In his analysis, vexing matters of justice, or the difficult moral calculus of the greatest good for the greatest number, are superseded by attention to the purely expressive function of punishment.

For Foucault and others, the prison—not the scaffold—best communicates the modern disposition of power.[15] Notably, it is Scott's most romantic least historical—fiction that embodies the opposition Foucault sees as central to the history of the direction and management of punishment: the bloody theater of physical proof in the medieval works gives way to the pervasive yet private and seemingly gentle control of behavior in *Redgauntlet*. That this movement is wholly accomplished within the romances should make clear to us the latent vitality of the older, more violent notion. And in assessing the inchoate workings of these deeply felt desires in our present culture, we would do well to note that Foucault's work (as Michael Ignatieff points out) triumphs brilliantly over the deterministic cultural and perceptual limits it seems to posit.[16]

The bearing Scott's romances have on the actual history of punishment does indeed suggest that wishes forcefully shape the ways we habitually think of the subject. The exotic novels and *Redgauntlet* assume rather than test authority. This assurance dispels the ambiguity or discomfort of such novels as *Rob Roy* or *The Heart of Midlothian*. Instead of critically evaluating differing justifications of punishment, the romances project the emotional satisfaction to be realized in carefully staged symbolic acts of justice and power. But the troubled, irresolute quality of Scott's realistic punishment scenes largely explains the seductive power of the confident, decisive scenes of the exotic tales and *Redgauntlet*; it is in such works as *Old Mortality* that we are informed of the complex and disturbing problems that lend great urgency in the late romances to the expression of our wishes. More importantly, the uncertain wisdom of the early Waverley novels provides us with a critical perspective on the attractive qualities of the later works. Even wishful ideas, after all, may have real consequences; as Bertrand de Jouvenel maintains, power grows under the cover of ideas we entertain about it.[17] We often find it difficult to believe that our understanding can be effectual against such forces. But in Scott's realistic novels, we are equipped to separate the cover of ideas from the power that is cloaked; we then see emerge from the romances ideas of power that buttress power's actual workings.

CHAPTER ONE

The Lesson of *Waverley*

————·•◄∞►•·————

The true practical question therefore is, What circumstance
it is that combines efficacy with severity of punishment?—
and this seems to be, *its being agreeable to the feelings of
natural justice, or having the concurrence of the public senti-
ment in its favour.* . . . Up to the tone of public feeling against
any criminal act, the severity of the punishment may be increased with effect:—beyond that point, it cannot be *forced*
with effect; nor, we might add, with propriety.
>—Sir Samuel Romilly

IN his *Second Treatise*, Locke argues that the right to punish—held by each person in a state of nature—is freely given up
for the public good in civil society. The distinctive power of the
state, then, resides in its right to make laws enforced by penalties—including the penalty of death.[1] Perhaps it is a power the
Waverley novels uphold more easily than Locke would approve.
Scott's heroes generally realize that the virtues of an established,
stable order depend upon the individual's surrender to (and for)
that order. As Alexander Welsh argues, they affirm civil society
through inaction or through a scrupulous attention to the proper
line of action. Their many appeals to the state's power underscore a
firm commitment to efface their private authority.[2] But the dimensions of this surrender exact a cost. Heroes like Edward Waverley
nearly disappear as the gap between them and the state steadily
widens.

Given the unequal relationship between individual citizens and
the state that is inherent in Scott's conception of the social contract, to what extent is it necessary or possible for the state to

determine the guilt of those it punishes? Or, more broadly put, is the state responsible for justice as well as for its own security? Certainly Locke stresses the responsibilities of government. The *Second Treatise* concerns the people's right to self-defense (i.e., rebellion) more than it concerns the government's right to punish.[3] Injustice severs the contractual obligations the individual has freely accepted and brings all to a state of war: "*Force without Right, upon a Man's Person, makes a State of War*, both where there is, and is not, a common Judge."[4] Yet, despite Scott's interest in past uprisings, this revolutionary side of Locke seems barely relevant to the Waverley novels of the post-1688 world. For example, in *Redgauntlet: A Tale of the Eighteenth Century* Scott has Dr. Grumball—a foolish, antiquated Jacobite—espouse royalist principles against the "blasphemous, atheistical, and anarchical tenets of Locke" (chap. 22, p. 399). Grumball's comic rebelliousness in defiance of a securely established Hanoverian government indicates that for Scott, Locke's radicalism had become a strictly historical issue; the revolution of 1688 was, after all, a special case—more of a final settlement than a tentative compromise.[5]

But if Scott's belief in the rightness and endurance of that settlement makes the *Second Treatise* a safer document than Locke intended, it does not remove from it all discomforting ideas. The state's rightful possession of power carries with it difficult responsibilities concerning the punishment and protection of its citizens. In this respect, the *Second Treatise* provides a context to help us understand both the threat of punishment and the grounds upon which that threat was realized and justified in Scott's time. To some extent, Locke eases the government's burden of responsibility by narrowing his sense of justice—by making justice a practical issue rather than an abstract ideal. His discussion of the contractual obligations implicit in one's participation in civil society eventually leads to a deterrence theory of punishment; for the contract depends upon an agreed system of mutual benefit, not an absolute or fixed right. In the late eighteenth and early nineteenth centuries, deterrence stood at the center of thought concerning punishment as utilitarians came to dominate debates over the reform of the criminal law. But their particular emphasis on deterrence hardly reduced the ambiguity expressed in the means of deterring. As Scott was to discover, a utilitarian act of punishment may be spoiled by running against intuitive notions of fairness.

For most readers, there is this apparent—indeed dramatic— unevenness of justice in *Waverley*: Scott's hero gets off with a beautiful wife and a large estate; the hero's friend is tortured and killed. The novelist's efforts to explain or justify the discrepancy help us locate his position in the contemporary debate over the reform of the criminal law. But, more importantly, his efforts teach us much about the problematic nature of utilitarian justifi- cations of punishment. Scott's uncertain authorial perspective on Fergus's execution betrays something other than artistic clum- siness. It betrays a nagging, unresolved dissatisfaction with the limited character of the debate in which he participates. Somehow that debate makes justice too small a matter. Questions of security and the general public good outweigh the more abstract concerns of fairness and human sympathy, but those latter qualities retain enough strength to undermine faith in the former. Scott could not comfortably disregard justice in favor of measurable virtues. For him, the greatest good for the greatest number was not so easily calculable. In this respect, Scott seems closely akin to most British novelists who concern themselves with broad social and historical subjects. The dramatic qualities of fiction, the human sympathies that it seems inevitably to enlist, make a Moll Flanders, a Jonathan Wild, or even a Fagin too weighty as human beings to place on a small scale of value. Bentham's objection to considering justice as a significant factor in matters of the state's responsibility sug- gests the reduction Scott and others find so vexing: "What is it that we are to understand by justice: and why not happiness . . . [instead of] justice?"[6] As many readers have found (and Scott may have sensed), it is precisely the idea of justice that makes the final happiness of Waverley so unconvincing or even distasteful.

Edward Waverley is the first of many Scott heroes to feel keenly the individual's vulnerability. Waverley, a young, inexperienced, slightly foolish sort, finds himself charged with high treason by Major Melville, the stern representative of the Hanoverian gov- ernment of 1745. Mr. Morton, a local clergyman, observes Mel- ville's examination of Waverley and attempts to counter the magis- trate's determined skepticism. Although good friends, Morton and

Melville are predisposed to radically different interpretations of Waverley's case. Morton has led a relatively easeful, rural life. He is not inclined to assume the worst of men. But he is not the magistrate. Melville sees little reason for extensive charity: "He was vigilant by profession, and cautious from experience, had met with much evil in the world, and therefore, though himself an upright magistrate and an honourable man, his opinions of others were always strict, and sometimes unjustly severe" (chap. 32, p. 162).[7]

But Melville can hardly be charged with unreasonable severity in his judgment and treatment of Waverley. Incidents and documents together with Waverley's family history conspire to indict the hero of high treason. Indeed, Waverley's "hasty review of his own conduct convinced him he might have great difficulty in establishing his innocence to the satisfaction of others" (chap. 31, p. 156). Yet even this consciousness of his guilty appearance hardly prepares him for the weight of circumstance that bears against him.

Melville reminds him of a "trifling commission" he gave Sergeant Houghton: to send some books of "elegant literature" to Tully-Veolan. Waverley's officious tutor, the nonjuring clergyman Mr. Pembroke, had seen fit to include two ponderous, treasonable volumes of his own composition with those Waverley had requested. Flora's poem on the death of Captain Wogan is also in Waverley's possession; it poses a striking likeness in its narrative to the seeming progress of Waverley's actions in the Highlands. The hero is visibly struck by the coincidence. Letters from the Waverley family provide Melville with further grounds for suspicion, for the inference he draws from them is far different from what Waverley expects. The letters Waverley does not receive add to his difficulty. Colonel Gardiner's requests for Waverley's return have been (we learn later) intercepted by the outlaw, Donald Bean Lean. And finally, untrue but not unfounded rumors of Waverley's acceptance of Balmawhapple's rebellious toast lead to the hero's overwhelming frustration: "Beset and pressed on every hand by accusations, in which gross falsehoods were blended with such circumstances of truth as could not fail to procure them credit,—alone, unfriended, and in a strange land, Waverley almost gave up his life and honour for lost, and, leaning his head upon his hand, resolutely refused to answer any further questions,

since the fair and candid statement he had already made had only
served to furnish arms against him" (chap. 31, pp. 159–60).

So by the midpoint of the novel, well before joining forces with
Fergus in behalf of the Pretender, Waverley finds himself en-
meshed in, and threatened by, circumstances he cannot explain.
The appearance of guilt is strong, despite the fact that Waverley's
first efforts—from the earliest news of rebellion and the suggestion that he is suspected to be part of that rebellion—are to verify
the contract he holds with the established government: "he was
aware that unless he meant at once to embrace the proposal of Fergus Mac-Ivor, it would deeply concern him to leave this suspicious
neighborhood without delay, and repair where his conduct might
undergo a satisfactory examination" (chap. 28, p. 140). Even if he
is to take arms in service to the Stuarts, he must first "clear his
own character by shewing that he had taken no step to this purpose, as seemed to be falsely insinuated, during his holding the
commission of the reigning monarch" (chap. 28, p. 141).

Despite these efforts, it is clear that Waverley imperfectly appreciates the extent of his surrender to civil government. Locke,
we should remember, stresses the responsibilities of citizenship
as well as of government. Waverley dismisses Colonel Gardiner's
early, gentle warnings as a "prejudiced and ill-judged suspicion"
(chap. 14, p. 67). And he petulantly resigns his commission in response to the colonel's final, direct orders. Such civil indiscretion
proves a serious offense, for it suggests Waverley's unwillingness to fulfill one-half of an agreement he has freely accepted. His
"magnanimous epistle" of resignation is the object of an unchar-
acteristically harsh, sarcastic tone on the part of Scott toward his
hero (chap. 25, p. 126).

Waverley, however, does have his defender, albeit a rather in
effectual one against Melville. The kindly Mr. Morton scrambles
from position to position in an attempt to make a case for the
accused. Morton first pleads for mercy on Waverley's behalf. But
Melville answers—in good utilitarian form—that mercy is best left
to God after man has exacted his worldly punishment: "mercy to
a criminal may be gross injustice to the community." Morton then
claims that guilt must be evaluated in relation to the moral motive that inspires it. But when that guilt is for the highest crimes,

Melville counters, it must not be so easily dismissed—for private virtues or values remain insubstantial abstractions against the concrete demands of political security: "If visionary chivalry and imaginary loyalty come within the predicament of high treason, I know no court in Christendom . . . where they can sue out their Habeas Corpus." Finally Morton takes the line Waverley himself has offered: "I cannot see that this youth's guilt is at all established to my satisfaction" (chap. 32, pp. 162–64).

But the burden of proof rests with Waverley, not the state, and the evidence sufficiently satisfies Melville, who fears Waverley "has brought himself within the compass of an halter."[8] Blackstone's warning on the dangers of naïveté applies to Waverley's case. No man, writes Blackstone, should assume that the criminal law has only abstract significance for his own life: "The infirmities of the best among us, the vices and ungovernable passions of others, the instability of all human affairs, and the numberless unforeseen events, which the compass of a day may bring forth, will teach us (upon a moment's reflection) that to know with precision what the laws of our country have forbidden, and the deplorable consequences to which a willful disobedience may expose us, is a matter of universal concern."[9] Apparently, even without "willful disobedience," the unforeseen events brought forth within the "compass of a day" can bring one like Waverley within the "compass of an halter." Ironically, Scott edges toward the moral he had found (nine years earlier) so repugnant in William Godwin's *Caleb Williams*: "the moral proposed . . . seems to be, not that a man guilty of theft or murder is in some danger of being hanged; but that, by a strange concurrence of circumstances, he may be regularly conducted to the gallows for theft or murder which he has never committed."[10]

The "mischievous" implications of this proposition are clearly at work on the hero of Scott's novel. At the time of Waverley's arrest and the government's first accusation against him, Morton's third line of defense—that Waverley's guilt is not sufficiently established—is strictly correct, yet clearly inadequate. Its inadequacy sets up a further chain of circumstances that more powerfully implicate the hero. Partly because Morton's early defense goes uncredited, Waverley becomes what Melville thinks he is; therefore, Waverley must ultimately be saved by a version of the clergyman's second defense: that the motive may excuse or qualify guilty actions. Colonel Talbot, an old friend of the Waverley family and a man of unquestioned devotion to the established government, eventually offers such a version in the most practical, political terms.[11] Talbot mixes the mercy of Morton and the prudence of Melville in his assessment of Waverley's case.[12] He maintains that some rebels, no doubt, will suffer for their actions. But not all need suffer. As Locke puts it: "even the guilty are to be spared, where it can prove no prejudice to the innocent."[13]

Certainly Talbot considers all the guilty subject to just punishment, but (as I will show in chapter 6) government may best preserve its strength by not expending it. Whatever inequality there may be in the uneven exercise of punishment demonstrates such pragmatic mercy as Locke recommends. The rough, commonsense character of Talbot's remarks suggests that government should not be zealous in its demands for justice. Strict justice, Talbot observes, can be too severe and too mean a master: "Where the guilty are so numerous, clemency must be extended to far the greater number; and I have little doubt of procuring a remission for you, provided we can keep you out of the claws of justice till she has selected and gorged upon her victims; for in this, as in other cases, it will be according to the vulgar proverb, 'First come first served'" (chap. 62, pp. 289–90). For Talbot, punishment is, no doubt, sometimes necessary, but it is always unpleasant.

Talbot's unbending severity toward Fergus demonstrates the force of necessity. He well understands that the execution of Waverley would serve no purpose. The young man is "tired of the trade of war"—hardly an example of rebellion for the dissatisfied to follow (chap. 62, p. 290). Nor does Waverley pose a future threat to the government. Flora's mildly contemptuous yet accurate description of his character makes it clear that this hero is a safe man to leave alive: "high and perilous enterprize is not Waverley's forte" (chap. 52, p. 250). But such enterprise does characterize Fergus:

> Colonel Talbot owned that he could not conscientiously use any influence in favour of that unfortunate gentleman. "Justice, which demanded some penalty of those who had wrapped the whole nation in fear and in mourning, could not have selected a fitter victim. . . . That he was brave, generous, and possessed many good qualities, only

rendered him more dangerous; that he was enlightened and accomplished, made his crime the less excusable; that he was an enthusiast in a wrong cause, only made him more fit to be its martyr. Above all, he had been the means of bringing many hundreds of men into the field, who, without him, would never have broken the peace of the country." (Chap. 67, p. 318)

The government's mercy cannot extend to those who, like Fergus, consciously and determinedly repudiate the existing contract implicitly accepted by the people for their own good.

Talbot's role as Waverley's protector, therefore, does not call into question his loyal and effective service to the established government. We must remember his flexibility and tact when we consider his position regarding Fergus's punishment. Talbot's condemnation of the Highland chief partakes of none of his usual anti-Scottish bias. He presents the case in a detailed, coherent, and convincing manner. Fergus's romantic ambitions, Talbot reminds us, have led to real death and suffering. We might remember that Waverley, once in the midst of battle, feels a profound sense of betrayal in the act of rebellion. Indeed, the killing of Colonel Gardiner seems to him an act of parricide. So Fergus's guilt is unquestioned. The consequences of that guilt are profound. And the threat of his continued life to the established government is real. Clearly, Fergus stands as the fittest victim of the severest punishment.

The language of the passage I have quoted above betrays Scott's endorsement of Talbot's position. Talbot speaks as if Fergus's crimes and punishment are completed actions. Talbot speaks not as a character at a specific, dramatic moment in a novel but rather as an author talking in his own voice. This identification is striking and curious, for Scott immediately disavows Talbot's position. A return to the simple present tense in Talbot's speech signals the coming separation of author from character: "I repeat it," said the colonel, "though heaven knows with a heart distressed for him as an individual, that this young gentleman has studied and fully understood the desperate game which he has played. He threw for life or death, a coronet or a coffin; and he cannot now be permitted, with justice to the country, to draw stakes, because the dice have gone against him" (chap. 67, pp. 318–19).

The immediate moment presses Fergus to death—to a coffin.

The colonel's convincing justification of punishment begins to take shape in the exercise of punishment. But punishment is more easily seconded as an abstraction. Neither Waverley nor the reader looks upon the actual horrors of Fergus's execution. Such a scene would surely test Talbot's reasoned dismissal of mercy: the punishment for high treason (an English law as Fergus points out) involves disemboweling, quartering, and beheading the convicted traitor. This concrete reality is too terrible to gain Scott's assent. Scott is careful to distance himself from Talbot's position as the consequences of that position become clear: "Such was the reasoning of those times, held even by brave and humane men towards a vanquished enemy. Let us devoutly hope, that, in this respect at least, we shall never see the scenes, or hold the sentiments, that were general in Britain Sixty Years since" (chap. 67, p. 319).

But the "reasoning of those times" is not so distant from Scott's own reasoning. Scott does not intend to question the necessity of the execution, just its gruesome staging. In 1817 (less than three years after the publication of *Waverley*), Scott takes a very Talbot-like stand on the case of a very Fergus-like victim. His "History of Europe, 1815" (written for the *Edinburgh Annual Register*) passes judgment on one General Labedoyere, who took up Napoléon's cause against Louis XVIII upon the former's return from Elba. Scott first calls attention to the "apology ingeniously urged in the criminal's behalf":

> Still young he [Labedoyere] had never served except under the colours of Napoleon. He had known Louis XVIII. only ten months. The first sovereign, whose abdication appeared to him only a sacrifice dictated by necessity, re-appeared suddenly before him. . . . It awakened affections which had been but ill extinguished. The illusion of the military glory—of the former power of the prince, rendered in the eyes of some of his partisans greater by his misfortunes and his exile, acted on an ardent and elevated imagination, which easily fancies the dictates of duty to be obeyed, even at the very moment in which the most sacred duties are trampled on. It must be confessed . . . that the multiplied changes of government have shaken, and have sometimes had the effect, during these 25 years, of rendering doubtful in France the notions of morality on the legitimacy of princes and the fidelity of subjects.

Scott, however, will accept no such apologies; he sounds very much like Talbot as he upholds the logic of accountability and the appropriateness of severity:

> While these facts are admitted, it ought to be remembered that the welfare of society depends upon repressing crimes against the state . . . and that if the doctrine of allegiance had become vague and doubtful in France, it was of the last consequence that it should be confirmed by a solemn example. . . . The criminal was conducted in a carriage to the plain of Grenelles, and there shot by a detachment of *gens d'armes*. He died with great firmness; and . . . while it is a crime for a soldier to betray his trust, or a subject to rebel against his sovereign, his execution must be considered as amply deserved.[14]

I have quoted this passage at length because it so closely parallels passages from *Waverley*, and thereby clarifies our sense of Scott's identification with Talbot's judgment.[15] It seems that Talbot correctly insists upon the execution of Fergus, but he fails (along with his author) to account sufficiently for the sympathies inspired by severe, public punishment. Fergus becomes grander in defeat than in attempt. Scott's abrupt move away from Talbot arises from his sense of an awkwardness in the dramatic act of execution. Punishments are designed to convey messages, but a faulty design can lead to unanticipated or undesirable results.[16] Even Labedoyere's relatively modest execution, Scott notes, "attracted much compassion" for the victim.[17]

In this respect, Scott's position as a novelist is roughly analogous to the position of those who make and enforce laws. Scenes of punishment—whether real or fictional—may easily and inadvertently evoke radical interpretations: the object of punishment can become the object of sympathy; the society that punishes can become the real criminal. Radical novelists such as William Godwin exploited these possibilities. The unjustly condemned, suffering prisoner is a staple figure in Jacobin fiction. But the conservative Scott could hardly be pleased with the turn his scene of punishment takes: Fergus states that his defense would be the government's condemnation; it so happens that his condemnation becomes his final (and perhaps most effective) defense.

Scott surely understood in principle the contrary effects to which the exercise of punishment made government liable. Not only did

he have the Jacobin model to learn from, but he could take note of a
considerable body of argument over the practical advantages and
problems of severity. This debate was sharpened by (but not limited to) efforts to reform Great Britain's criminal law—especially
that portion of the law concerning capital punishment. A crucial
period in the history of this reform effort is contemporary with
Scott's career as a novelist.[18]

Waverley is, of course, a novel of a historic rebellion. But Fergus's crime and punishment should not be divorced from the state
of Great Britain in 1814. Any crime can be seen as an act of rebellion, and in 1814 practically any crime could subject its perpetrator
to the punishment of death. The most vigorous reform efforts in
Scott's day centered on this extraordinarily wide extension of the
death penalty, and the meaning that the law and its application
communicated to the public. The problematic issues raised by this
debate provide a context for a further understanding of Scott's
presentation of Fergus's death and Waverley's escape. In addition,
Scott's intelligent but irresolute handling of utilitarian, reformist
assumptions suggests a deeply ambivalent attitude toward the
prevailing wisdom of his day.

As I have noted, in Scott's time deterrence was generally assumed to be punishment's justifying purpose. By 1814 this assumption had been securely established. Locke based his justification
of capital punishment on its power to deter and to protect.[19] The
commonsense approach to moral problems by such philosophers
as Francis Hutcheson and Adam Ferguson typified a resistance
to the difficult abstractions of a retributivist position, which asserts that justice alone is the final justification of punishment. For
Hutcheson, "the end of punishment is the general safety."[20] For
Ferguson, writing over twenty years later, in 1769, "the object of
punishment is to correct the guilty, and to deter others."[21] Blackstone's remarks on "the *end*, or final cause of human punishments"
are characteristic in their emphasis on the unavoidable (but acceptable) limitations of worldly justice: "This is not by way of
atonement or expiation for the crime committed; for that must be
left to the just determination of the Supreme Being; but as a pre-
caution against future offenses of the same kind. This is effected
three ways: either by amendment of the offender himself; . . . by
deterring others by the dread of his example from offending in

the like way; . . . or, lastly, by depriving the party injuring of the power to do future mischief."[22] Such an emphasis on the practical necessity of punishment prepared a receptive audience for a 1767 English translation of Beccaria's *On Crimes and Punishments*. In *An Introduction to the Principles of Morals and Legislation* (1789) Bentham took Beccaria's lead and subjected the problem of punishment to a more thorough and detailed utilitarian analysis.[23] By the time that *Waverley* was published, the utilitarian approach was so dominant that *The Cheap Magazine*—a Scottish publication for the "lower orders"—could invoke the spirit of Beccaria ("it is better to prevent crimes than to punish them") with the assurance that his ideas had some common currency.[24]

None of this is to deny that serious disagreement did exist, but most such disagreements arose from within—not from without—the utilitarian camp. By the time of the publication of *Waverley*, three distinct positions on capital punishment laws and their administration had emerged. The three can be represented by Martin Madan's doctrine of severity, William Paley's defense of the status quo, and Sir Samuel Romilly's parliamentary efforts to bring Beccaria's and Bentham's principles to bear on the criticism and reform of the English criminal law. All three addressed a peculiar fact: as the number of capital statutes increased, the exercise of those statutes decreased. More criminals were subject to hanging. Fewer actually hanged.

Martin Madan's *Thoughts on Executive Justice* (1785) argued the most reactionary (and generally least acceptable) thesis on the state of the law. Madan considered prevention "the great end of all legal severity." Punishments not meant to deter are worthless and therefore cruel.[25] But whereas Beccaria argued that the certainty of punishment should alleviate its severity, Madan counseled for both certainty and severity. If a law specifies death as the penalty for a crime, then that penalty should be exacted. Madan placed considerable trust in the terror that would result from the strict administration of existing statutes. In short, he accepts the state of the law, but attacks judicial weakness for undercutting the law. The legislature acts, Madan insists, with clear and reasonable intent; the judges subvert that intent: "I must confess, that my apprehension is at a loss to conceive the idea of the *Legislative* power of a country, enacting a Law for any *purpose* whatsoever, which they do not mean to be executed."[26]

Madan invokes the duke's speech from *Measure for Measure* on the results of relaxed statutes ("in time the rod / Becomes more mock'd than fear'd") without the least acknowledgment of the moral ambiguities Shakespeare introduces as a consequence of this attitude. Madan's ideal magistrate might well be one as literal minded and cynical as Shakespeare's deputy Angelo or Scott's magistrate Melville. Certainly Talbot believes in a selective severity Madan could hardly allow.

William Paley shares Madan's faith in the wisdom of the legislature. But Paley detects that wisdom in the very discrepancy between the law and its administration that appalls Madan. In his *Moral and Political Philosophy* (also 1785), Paley maintains that the many laws threatening death are intended to allow judges the widest possible range of action. He would agree with Madan that it is England's "happiness, that, as crimes have arisen there have been laws made to repress them."[27] But he would insist that threats need not be consistently realized to be threatening. Uncertainty has its own terrors: "By the number of statutes creating capital offenses, [the law] sweeps into the net every crime which under any possible circumstances, may merit the punishment of death; but when execution of this sentence comes to be deliberated upon, a small proportion of each class are singled out. . . . By this expedient, few actually suffer death, whilst the dread and danger of it hangs over the crimes of many. The tenderness of the law cannot be taken advantage of."[28] Paley is a great defender of things as they are. For him, the law's discretionary power solidifies the basis of power upon which the practice of punishment depends.[29]

The moral basis for the law's discretionary breadth, however, seems very weak indeed. Paley leads himself, as Talbot leads Scott, into some tenuous positions. Like Talbot, Paley refuses to proportion punishment to guilt; rather, he adjusts punishment "to the difficulty and necessity of preventing" crime.[30] To some extent, Paley's rigorous, utilitarian logic works against itself. The naive confidence apparent throughout his chapter on punishment exposes the moral deficiencies utilitarian thought is liable to. Not only does he deny any necessary relationship between the degree of guilt and the extent of punishment, but he is also quite comfortable with the possibility that the innocent may suffer under the law. As I have shown, Waverley finds the possibilities disturbingly real. He could take no solace from the selfless ideal of individual sacrifice so easily put forth by Paley: "He who falls by a mistaken sentence, may be considered as falling for his country; whilst he suffers under the operation of those rules, by the general effect and tendency of which the welfare of the community is maintained and upholden."[31] The idea that the innocent may serve as effectively as the guilty for the purposes of punishment is one that later utilitarians have taken care to disavow, or, at least, to skirt.[32] But Paley makes no effort to do either; he makes a virtue of what he sees as a necessity.

In the balance of evil between crime and punishment, Talbot allows a man's life more weight than Paley does. The colonel's efforts in Waverley's behalf attest to more than simple loyalty to the son of an old benefactor. Talbot concerns himself as much with the unnecessary evil of punishment as with its necessary evil. Furthermore, his distinction between disgraceful and criminal actions suggests an awareness (nearly absent in Paley) of the disturbance to which punishment subjects the entire community, for he recognizes that "unfortunate gentlemen" are part of that community. In some respects, Talbot's utilitarianism (as well as Scott's) resembles Bentham's.[33] Surely Talbot would agree that punishment should guard against crime "at as cheap a rate possible." And a large portion of such cost-efficient punishment depends upon the management of the execution itself. In addition, Talbot, like Bentham, recognizes the futility of a punishment at odds with the public's sympathy.[34] The society that has no will to punish, will not punish: "Government are desirous at present to intimidate the English Jacobites, among whom they can find few examples for punishment. This is a vindictive and timid feeling which will soon wear off, for, of all nations, the English are least bloodthirsty by nature. But it exists at present, and you [Waverley] must, therefore, be kept out of the way in the mean time" (chap. 62, p. 290).

Talbot's contention that the English lack a thirst for blood finds an odd confirmation of sorts in the kind of uneven or intermittent exercise of the numerous capital punishment statutes. It also, along with Bentham's remarks on the importance of the public's sympathy, leads us directly to the third—and eventually most persuasive—position on the gap between the law and its administration. By 1814, Sir Samuel Romilly—a friend of Bentham and an antagonist of Madan—had taken the first effective steps toward significant legislative reform of the criminal law. In opposition to Madan, Romilly accepted Beccaria's view that the certainty of punishment should alleviate its severity.[35] And in opposition to Paley, Romilly argued that the inconsistent application of the laws worked against the deterrent value of punishment. To his mind, public unease—not judicial weakness or legislative intent—led to the discrepancy between the letter and the administration of the law. Laws perceived as overly severe were rarely carried out.[36]

Romilly's sensitivity to the public's will was hardly unique. In 1821, the *Edinburgh Review* insisted the law had become a "dead letter" because it overreached the public's determination to enforce it: "The fact is, that persons are or may be more slow to prosecute a shoplifter—witnesses more unwilling to come forward— juries more anxious to acquit—and judges more prone to reprieve or pardon—than if the punishment were less severe."[37] In Scott's time, few people could defend the justice of killing a person for shoplifting over five shillings' worth of goods. Such a punishment would cast the law as the villain. The law could make no claim to justice or to necessity. Its continued existence would be called into question whenever it was exercised. Romilly points to the case of two boys, aged sixteen and seventeen, who were to be executed for forgery: "Was it possible that such spectacles as these could have any other effect than to produce, not obedience to the law, but compassion for the violators of it?"[38] Writing for the *Quarterly Review*, Robert Southey and John Rickman are quick to pick up the lesson and echo Romilly's point in their own conservative terms; the government cannot afford to inspire its most radical critics: "When the measure of punishment exceeds the offence, the laws are in contradiction to our natural sense of equity, and a hostile feeling toward them is excited, innocent and even honourable in its origin, but dangerous in its consequences."[39]

Romilly saw another danger in a possible backlash that might result from his own efforts. In a last attempt to resist reform, dead laws could be made—at times—to live. If the laws were demonstrably inadequate because they were not enforced, then they could be enforced instead of changed.[40] Madan's proposals could be resurrected as a conservative reaction to the reformers' zeal. The dangers of severity could be easily tested without altering the existing criminal laws.

Paley's apology for things as they are also proved to be amazingly durable. In fact, during Romilly's early parliamentary efforts, Paley's work was invoked by a member of the House of Lords as a "great national object to maintain" against the threat posed by a systematic reform of the criminal law. In a letter to Romilly, Dugald Stewart (Scott's old teacher) praises the statesman's attack on Paley, who seems (unaccountably to Stewart) an "oracle both in politics and in morals" to many Englishmen.[41]

This atmosphere of unresolved controversy extends throughout the career of the Author of *Waverley*. In his nonfiction, Scott's position regarding the reform of the criminal law seems clear enough, even if a bit sketchy: the death penalty is necessary, but it should only be exercised when necessary.[42] In a review article on a history of the crimes and punishment of a Gypsy band, Scott wrote that the tales it contains illustrate three "great doctrines": "that cruel and sanguinary laws usually overshoot their own purpose, drive to desperation these [*sic*] against whom they are levelled, and, by making man an object of chace [*sic*], convert him into a savage beast of prey."[43] Near the end of his life, in his *Letters on Demonology and Witchcraft*, Scott strikes a similar note in discussing the effects of an overly rigid exercise of severe laws; but in this case, he reflects specifically upon a situation closely akin to that presented in *Waverley*. Again we are reminded of the similarity between Scott and Talbot:

> Penal laws, like those of the middle ages denounced against witchcraft, may be at first hailed with unanimous acquiescence and approbation, but are uniformly found to disgust and offend at least the more sensible part of the public, when the punishments become frequent, and are relentlessly inflicted. Those against treason are no exception. Each reflecting government will do well to shorten that melancholy reign of terror, which perhaps must necessarily follow on the discovery of a plot, or the defeat of an insurrection. They ought not, either in humanity or policy, to wait till the voice of a nation calls to them, as Mecaenas to Augustus, "*Surge tandem, carnifex!*"[44]

Despite the assurance suggested by the above passages, Scott's imaginative difficulties regarding the issue of punishment are evidenced by the fact that only once again (in *The Heart of Midlothian*) does he fully present a scene of legal execution in a novel of the world after 1688. He generally finds extralegal means to deal with his postrevolutionary criminals and rebels. In his second novel, *Guy Mannering*, Dirk Hatteraick preempts the law's most unpleasant task by strangling his partner, Glossin, before hanging himself. The criminal, then, conveniently becomes his own punisher; the state and those who support it may be relieved of an unwanted responsibility.

In *The Myth of the State*, Ernst Cassirer reports an anecdote that may be used to underscore Scott's quandary with Fergus's punishment. Upon hearing Napoléon's orders for the execution of the Duke of Enghien, an adviser appeals to his prince: "C'est plus qu'un crime, C'est une faut!"[45] But even if Talbot were right that the execution of Fergus was no mistake, Scott might still find it a crime. The idea that such limited values of policy operate in deciding a person's fate proves upsetting. It is not only the judgment but the terms of the judgment that gnaw at him.

Perhaps in his first novel Scott stumbled upon the problematic issues of justice and expediency raised in the act of punishment. Certainly he moves away from the severed heads atop the gates of Carlisle with unseemly speed. The chapter immediately following the trial and execution of Fergus is titled "Dulce Domum," Home, Sweet Home. Waverley prepares for the peace and happiness that lie before him and his bride. Scott's own response to Waverley as a "sneaking piece of imbecility" may arise from the hero's disturbingly abrupt recovery.[46] For Scott, the lesson of *Waverley* was that fictions confront the real world—that the sympathies stirred by the punishment of Fergus disturb the vision of the settled, stable world Waverley so comfortably inherits.[47] In *Old Mortality* Scott at least implicitly acknowledges the pains that were exacted in establishing that order, and thereby he more fully explores the basis of established power.

CHAPTER TWO

Old Mortality and the Right to Punish

It is as true today as it was ten thousand years ago that a
Power from which the magic virtue has gone out, falls.
                                        —Bertrand de Jouvenel

IN no Scott novel are claims to authority made so unbendingly,
so emphatically, as they are in *Old Mortality*; yet in no other
Scott novel is power so suspect—so clearly asserted out of desperation, so clearly destructive. The conflict among competing
claims provides the Author of *Waverley* with material for his most
thorough exploration of the basis of political power and, in turn, of
revolution. And punishment—as an expression of power—takes
a central place in the narrative; in the midst of rebellion, the act
of punishment becomes a means to assert power or claim right.
Punishment effectively and dramatically expresses both of these
qualities.[1] Claverhouse, for example, maintains such supreme confidence in his power that he never questions its right. As a representative of the king (who represents God), Claverhouse sheds
blood without mercy or remorse; it suffices for him to make a fine
distinction in value between the life of a royalist and the life of a
rebel. As a direct representative of a rather more personal God,
the rebel leader John Balfour of Burley defends the assassination
of Archbishop Sharpe by calling it an "execution" or "a deed of
justice." Indeed, Burley assumes the act's rightness is confirmed
by its accomplishment: "Was not the execution itself a proof of our
warrant?" (chap. 21, p. 199).

   In *Waverley*, there is little such sense of balance between com-

peting claims. There the dominant impression concerning the rebellion is of unevenness, both in strength and in right. Edward
Waverley falls into his dreamlike opposition to the settled government and wakes up to the practical impossibility and moral
undesirability of revolution. The problem concerning punishment
in *Waverley*, then, becomes one of defining its justifying purpose
and controlling its message in terms of that purpose. Scott's perspective in that novel—his own satisfaction in the validity of the
Hanoverian order—makes it unnecessary to justify the power that
sanctions punishment. The right to punish, therefore, is secure
even though the purpose of punishment (or its effectiveness) is
open to question. The result, as I have shown, is an uncertain
commentary on the utilitarian assumptions that dominated debate
over punishment in the early nineteenth century.

   The uncertainty in *Old Mortality* is a more fundamental kind,
for in this novel Scott presents no clearly marked line of legitimate, established power. Nor does either side represent a securely
established power. If the Covenanters of 1679 are as hopelessly
undermanned (and as desperately fanatical) as the Jacobites of
1745, they at least represent a wide dissatisfaction that eventually deposes James II. And very unlike Waverley, the hero
of *Old Mortality* chooses his role: Henry Morton is a reluctant
rebel, but no less willful for his reluctance. Because history largely
affirms his choice (however belatedly), Morton's position serves to
define rightful authority in opposition to those, like Claverhouse
or Burley, who would claim arbitrary power, who would legitimize
murder—who would, in short, make executions of assassinations.
Against these false assumptions and claims, Morton represents
an authority dependent upon an agreement that cannot be pre-
empted; for him the right to punish is defensible only within a
system of law that promotes individual liberty in a state of civil
society. As John P. Farrell points out, Morton's tragedy is that
he must wait for history to form and solidify such a system before
he can enjoy its benefits.[2] In the chaotic state of late Stuart rule,
acts of punishment by either side function merely as acts of war
disguised by a presumption of moral or religious superiority.

   David Hewitt notes the modern reader's difficulty in pinning
down the specific meaning of Morton's abstract claims of right and

liberty; he goes on to insist that such claims can be best defined by reference to particular political controversies in Great Britain during the early nineteenth century.[3] Like Graham McMaster's *Scott and Society*, Hewitt's essay does much to clarify Scott's engagement with the immediate world about him. My analysis of *Waverley* indicates my sympathy for such efforts. But we should be careful not to overcorrect for a naive criticism that removes the subject of historical fiction from contemporary reference.[4] Scott gains perspective on the present by seeing it in relation to the past. To be more specific, Henry Morton represents what can be seen in retrospect as the force of a hard-won historical progress—a progress that makes punishment subject to some degree of rational control or systematic limitation within a firmly established political order.[5]

In establishing his position, Morton deliberately makes himself subject to harm. He places himself in dangerous situations and he resolutely accepts the consequences of his actions. When he chooses to shelter Burley against government troops, he does so with full knowledge of the risk he takes: "the punishment of the law shall fall upon myself, as in justice it should" (chap. 5, p. 39). Nor does Morton's resolve to take things upon his own head weaken as his hopes of saving his head decrease. Bothwell (the trooper who arrests him) suggests that Morton may be delivered from the law by a fine upon his uncle's estate; but this prospect only vexes Morton: "I wish to Heaven, if I escape a capital punishment, that the penalty may be of a kind I could bear in my own person" (chap. 9, p. 81). Even as he prepares to face Claverhouse, Morton will not plead his ignorance of Burley's crime in order to explain away his own: "I am at least uncertain whether, even if I had known the crime, I could have brought my mind, under all the circumstances, to refuse a temporary refuge to the fugitive" (chap. 10, p. 97).

A seeming contradiction is apparent in Morton's behavior, for he is simultaneously a good citizen and a deliberately disobedient one. On one hand, Morton accepts the necessity of an authority separate from himself; he does not claim the right to be a judge in his own cause. Under certain conditions, he will accept punishment. On the other hand, he does not allow that necessity to contradict his sense of justice; he denies the right of those who judge him. He will invite punishment by his disobedience. The good citizen and the rebel may be seen as consistent with each other if we enlarge our idea of Morton's personal sense of right and see his individual assertion as founded upon fundamental laws of all legitimate authority. Morton possesses a firm albeit limited sense of natural law and its relationship to the ends of government. But Morton's sense of natural law—despite his occasional reference to "Heaven" or the "Almighty"—does not depend upon divine authority. Nor does Morton express a belief in a detailed, complicated system of natural law. Rather he works from a fairly secular, rational, and minimalist conception of natural law. H. L. A. Hart provides a brief and illuminating discussion of the modern notion of natural law disentangled from a "metaphysical setting." Hart's attention to the "approximate equality" of men (i.e., even the strong are vulnerable to the violence of the weak) can serve to gloss much of Scott's political thought in *Old Mortality*: "This fact of approximate equality, more than any other, makes obvious the necessity for a system of mutual forbearance and compromise which is the base of both legal and moral obligation. Social life with its rules requiring such forbearance is irksome at times, but it is at any rate less nasty, less brutish, and less short than unrestrained aggression for beings thus approximately equal."[6]

Morton's first confrontation with Claverhouse helps to define his position more fully. Claverhouse—the military representative of government—has no apparent grasp of the government's role as servant to the people.[7] Claverhouse assumes his prince holds a right of command that cannot be limited by private persons. He acts consistently upon this assumption. Scott introduces Claverhouse as a character "formed in times of civil discord, when the highest qualities, perverted by party spirit and inflamed by habitual opposition, are too often combined with vices and excesses which deprive them at once of their merit and of their lustre" (chap. 12, p. 112). When Lady Margaret asks if there is no law to punish Cuddie Headrigg for his recusancy, Claverhouse replies, "I think I could find one" (chap. 12, p. 113). And Evandale expresses doubt that he can influence Claverhouse to extend mercy to Morton, for many such pleas made "on the mere score of humanity" have gone unattended (chap. 12, p. 120). It is important to note that Claverhouse's power to injure others is essentially unrelated to justice or to law. To put it another way, Claverhouse acts from a sense of the power he possesses, not from a concept of law that supports that power. In fact, he considers any law regarding the rebels irrelevant to his responsibility. The people have no rights in a dispute with their king.

Claverhouse holds to what is in 1679 a stubborn but fading notion of authority. James I had articulated often and at length the concept of the king's divine prerogative. And by doing so with impolitic insistency he encouraged the development of an opposing, more democratic ideology.[8] (Similarly, Morton's own political awakening can be seen as a response to aggressive injustice.) The civil war revived absolutist doctrines in various forms. Whereas Robert Filmer asserted a basis for the king's power in God's will (and became the target of Locke's *First Treatise*), other (more successful) thinkers such as Samuel Pufendorf, Anthony Ascham, and Thomas Hobbes secularized the virtues of submission.[9] According to these theorists, although might and right are not synonymous, the latter is too vague an idea to maintain against the concrete influence of the former. In Hobbes's terms, Claverhouse inflicts harm as an act of hostility—not as an act of punishment: "For the Punishments set down in the Law, are to Subjects, not to Enemies."[10] Yet such acts of hostility are not necessarily illegitimate; as I will show in chapters 5 and 6, punishment as defined by Hobbes requires one's implied prior assent to the original charter of the state. With respect to the strenuously dissenting victims he kills, Claverhouse accurately expresses the government's position: England is at war with the rebels. By refusing to make the proper gestures of submission, the most radical Covenanters cut off all hopes for negotiation—for a process of law or fair treatment under the law. Even the moderate Duke of Monmouth rejects Morton's supremely moderate proposal for peace: "you must distinctly understand that I can only treat with supplicants, not with rebels" (chap. 30, p. 283).

Morton is unwilling to accept the role of enemy or rebel, but his uncomfortable neutrality as subject takes a decisive turn when he is brought before Claverhouse. He still lacks sympathy with the spirit of fanatical rebellion; "but his mind was still more revolted by the tyrannical and oppressive conduct of the government, the misrule, license, and brutality of the soldiery, the executions on the scaffold, the slaughters in the open field, the free quarters and exactions imposed by the military law, which placed the lives and fortunes of a free people on a level with Asiatic slaves" (chap. 13, p. 124). As this passage makes clear, Morton assumes his status as a free man in a legally constituted civil society. In addition, his reference to slaves reminds us of the relation of freedom to property; slaves, of course, own nothing—not even themselves. Any power that fails to grant Morton the status of a free man (a man with property in himself) forfeits its claim to legitimacy. Morton, therefore, rejects Claverhouse's Hobbesian presumption: " 'By what right is it, sir,' said he firmly, and without waiting till he was questioned,—'By what right is it that these soldiers have dragged me from my family, and put fetters on the limbs of a free man?' " Claverhouse maintains that his position commands sufficient authority, but Morton persists: "I will know whether I am in lawful custody, and before a civil magistrate, ere the charter of my country shall be forfeited in my person" (chap. 13, p. 128). Morton himself calls into question the legitimacy of Claverhouse's authority by invoking both his natural and civil rights as a free subject. In doing so he broadens his individual claims to include those made by all who suffer under arbitrary power.

In opposition to the government's identification of right with power, Morton puts forward a more liberal doctrine. Whereas Claverhouse and even Monmouth speak the language of Hobbes, Morton's diction echoes Locke.[11] Morton can oppose tyranny and remain a subject to rightful authority; for, as Locke puts it, "no body can desire to *have me in his Absolute Power*, unless it be to compel me by force to that, which is against the Right of my Freedom, *i.e.* to make me a Slave."[12] The individual's right to liberty—to dispose of his "Person, Actions, Possessions" free from the "arbitrary will of another"—stands as the "end of Law" for the entire community.[13] Again freedom is seen as inherent in property. And Morton's list of rights is as comprehensive as Locke's: his person, actions, and possessions cannot be forfeited without violating the charter of his country.

Morton's decision to join the rebels arises out of his concern to preserve liberty; he challenges government only to remind it of its responsibility. He refuses to submit to arbitrary power, yet he recognizes the moral complexity of this refusal; he has little confidence in the justice the Covenanters promise. Morton makes his characteristically deliberate choice not because of but despite Burley's enthusiasm for the Presbyterian effort:

> He doubted, indeed, greatly whether the present attempt was likely to be supported by the strength sufficient to ensure success, or by the wisdom and liberality of spirit necessary to make good use of the advantages that might be gained. Upon the whole, however, considering the wrongs he had personally endured, and those which he had seen daily inflicted on his fellow-subjects; meditating also upon the precarious and dangerous situation in which he already stood with relation to the government, he conceived himself, in every point of view called upon to join the body of Presbyterians already in arms. (Chap. 21, p. 198)

Regardless of the apparent necessity of his decision, however, Morton immediately qualifies his enlistment in the rebellion. He insists that in joining the uprising he does not sanction the event that initiated it—the killing of Sharpe. His moral reserve keeps his participation in the cause distinct from certain actions taken on behalf of that cause.

Such a distinction makes Morton an oddly conservative revolutionary. By refusing to affirm the Covenanters' power to punish, Morton strictly limits his claims against the established government. He pleads his rights as a freeborn citizen against the abuse of those rights by such representatives as Claverhouse. But he does not seek to regain those rights by establishing a new sovereign power. His reflections on joining the insurgents make it clear that Morton appreciates the moral as well as the military limitations of the rebel forces. As Judith Wilt observes, Morton speaks and fights "not to destroy the enemy but to establish conditions with them."[14] He hopes to moderate government policy, not overthrow the government.[15] In his examination before Claverhouse, Morton grants that "were he [Claverhouse] a civil officer of the law, I should know my duty was submission" (chap. 13, p. 129).

Again, Locke's *Second Treatise* (or at least a safe reading of it) can be used as a commentary on the realism of Morton's basically defensive position. Locke concedes the dangers inherent in opposing the crown: anarchy and confusion. But in extraordinary cases, self-preservation warrants disobedience: "*Force* is to be *op-*

posed to nothing, but to unjust and unlawful Force." [16] Hobbes also allows self-defense as a right, but he presumes a more contentious state where all is kept in order by strength. Locke's adjectives "unjust" and "unlawful" suggest the point of difference. In any case, self-defense for Locke need not constitute general rebellion.

For Locke, resistance becomes rebellion only when the acts of tyrannical power are widely perceived as threatening individual liberty. At that point, the revolutionary potential of an abused public is realized; government must bear the consequences of its misrule: "But if . . . these illegal Acts have extended to the Majority of the People . . . and they are perswaded in their Consciences, that their Laws, and with them their Estates, Liberties, and Lives are in Danger, and perhaps their Religion too, how they will be hindered from resisting illegal force, used against them, I cannot tell." [17] The uprising of 1679 anticipates but does not itself constitute such a decisive challenge to established government. We should remember here that *Two Treatises* was written well before the revolution, parts of it perhaps as early as the action that takes place in *Old Mortality*. Scott's hindsight, then, matches Locke's insight: numerous unchecked local acts of tyranny must eventually be felt as comprehensive attacks on liberty, and must be responded to as such. But surely Morton defines his own role in the rebellion as an attempt to put a just end to it. As Evandale recognizes, however, the "fanaticism and violent irritation of both parties" make war the only viable form of diplomacy (chap. 29, p. 269).

If Morton's acts of resistance are not in themselves revolutionary, they do lend credit to revolution. And if history justifies Morton, it does not do so in precisely the way he had planned. His principal frustration, in fact, arises from his inability to make actions agree with intentions. [18] Adam Ferguson's sense of the individual's "blindness" to specific future developments can be used to comment upon Morton's situation. For Ferguson, men don't make history; they stumble upon it. The complex of interests operating within a community denies the individual any controlling influence: "Men, in general, are sufficiently disposed to occupy themselves in forming projects and schemes: but he who would scheme and project for others, will find an opponent in every person who is disposed to scheme for himself." [19] The conflicts within the rebel camp between Morton and Burley or Poundtext and Macbriar illustrate the frustration inherent in "forming projects and schemes."

Intentions, therefore, have little to do with Morton's role in history. By refusing to surrender the first right of nature—self-defense—he poses a real but unshaped threat to tyrannical power. Morton's concept of rights encompasses more than he realizes—and more than a conservative such as Burke could ever allow.[20] The distinction between Morton's intent and his effect is important, for it deepens our sense of Scott's own conservatism. Morton's insistence upon his rights does lead him to battle against an established government. And the bloody skirmishes of 1679 are very much a part of the "bloodless" revolution of 1688.[21] But Scott's awareness and acceptance of the necessary violence that contributed to the revolution should not obscure Morton's moderate intent.[22] Indeed, Burke's description of the virtues necessary to reform read very much like a description of Morton's virtues:

> At once to preserve and to reform is quite another thing. When the useful parts of an old establishment are kept, and what is superadded is to be fitted to what is retained, a vigorous, steady, persevering attention, various powers of comparison and combination, and the resources of an understanding fruitful in expedients are to be exercised; they are to be exercised in a continued conflict with the combined force of opposite vices, with the obstinacy that rejects all improvement and the levity that is fatigued and disgusted with everything of which it is in possession.[23]

Whatever its merits, Morton's middle way between the forces of tyrannical government and fanatical rebellion proves awkward, for it aligns him with a world still unformed. In fact, it aligns him with a world he has not imagined.[24]

Clearly the "precarious and dangerous situation" Morton holds in relation to government is hardly less precarious or dangerous in relation to the opposition. Neither the unwarranted presumption of Claverhouse nor the ill-founded assumption of Burley claims Morton's assent. His difficult independence is apparent early. At the battle of Drumclog, Morton's first act once he is freed from government troopers is to help his rival escape from the Covenanters: "I will not trust Lord Evandale's life with these obdurate men."

Evandale's remark to Morton's servant Cuddie applies equally
well to Morton: "thy courtesy may cost thy life" (chap. 17, p. 169).

The "obdurate men" Morton eventually joins are much quicker
than Claverhouse to articulate their claims to authority, and they
are no less threatening for all their talk. They act from a conscious
desire to gain credit—not from an assurance of credit. Early in
the novel, Burley makes their aggressive ethic clear to Morton,
who resists it in terms that he will hold to throughout. Morton,
unaware of Sharpe's death, engages Burley on a subject of special
relevance to the fugitive. In their discussion, Burley shifts about
in an attempt to establish the moral justice of and legal right to
perform such acts as the killing of Sharpe. He finds the legal right
especially difficult to establish. Burley unintentionally concedes
that inspiration—his first proof of right—will hardly do: "And
think you that when some prime tyrant has been removed from
his place, that the instruments of his punishment can at all times
look back on their share in his downfall with firm and unshaken
nerves? Must they not sometimes even question the truth of that
inspiration which they have felt and acted under?" (chap. 6, p. 45).
Morton does not fail to call attention to Burley's uncharacteristic
admission of uncertainty as he separates natural law from mere
private enthusiasm: "I own I should strongly doubt the origin of
any inspiration which seemed to dictate a line of conduct contrary
to those feelings of natural humanity which Heaven has assigned
to us as the general law of our conduct" (chap. 6, p. 45).

Burley puts aside his temporary lapse into self-doubt and counters Morton by implicitly claiming scriptural authority for his
actions. Such authority liberates one from the "dungeon-house of
the law." Morton, however, wants no such liberation. He refuses to
acknowledge a distinction between inspiration and Scripture as a
basis for authority when the latter depends upon an interpretation
guided by the "spirit within." He seeks a broad basis of authority
that to some extent harmonizes civil law with natural law. The "re-
straints of legal magistracy, of national law, and even of common
humanity" must not be rejected on the basis of "an inward light"
(chap. 6, p. 46).

Morton's stubbornness forces Burley to a more particular and
more effective, historically grounded line of argument: it is the

government that has "rejected all law, both divine and civil, and . . . now persecute[s] us for adherence to the Solemn League and Covenant between God and the kingdom of Scotland." On the issue of persecution, Morton can hardly refute Burley; he can, however, withhold his commitment to battle against it: "You will excuse me from engaging myself either in your cause or in controversy" (chap. 6, p. 46). It seems that for Morton, Burley's claims to rightful authority cannot be granted merely on the grounds of the other side's wrongs. The right to punish, therefore, needs more than a negative basis.

As I have noted, Morton and Burley return to the subject of punishment upon Morton's provisional enlistment in the rebellion. On this occasion, their discussion has a concrete point of reference: Morton now knows that Burley is responsible for the death of Sharpe. Yet Burley's defense in this second encounter is more focused and assured. He has shirked the odium of responsibility and embraced the opportunity of responsibility. He proclaims his act as an expression of just and legitimate power. He will not allow Morton to join the rebellion and still maintain a distance from the killing without a direct and forceful challenge to his principles: "You are of opinion that the justice of an execution consists, not in the extent of the sufferer's crime, or in his having merited punishment, or in the wholesome and salutary effect which that example is likely to produce upon other evil-doers, but hold that it rests solely in the robe of the judge, the height of the bench, and the voice of the doomster? Is not just punishment justly inflicted, whether on the scaffold or the moor?" (chap. 21, p. 199).

But Burley continues to beg what is for Morton the essential question. He fails to keep the justice of an act separate from the right to act. It is not enough that punishment is deserved or is of practical value. It is not enough that Sharpe's crimes "merited" punishment, or that his death might have a positive influence on others. Without a system of laws there are no punishments—only acts of hostility. Even in war, Morton notes, men need not violate common principles of humanity: "I join a cause supported by men engaged in open war, which it is proposed to carry on according to the rules of civilised nations" (chap. 21, p. 200). As Ferguson puts it, "even the best qualities of men, their candour, as well as their resolution, may operate in the midst of their quarrels." In fact, "war does not always proceed from an intention to injure."[25] The killing of Sharpe, however, can hardly be described in such a way; it constitutes an "act of violence" that flouts Morton's rules of war, as well as any rules of law that might be supposed to empower executioners. Only in the position he scornfully attributes to Morton does Burley unwittingly make the crucial shift from justice to right; the robe of the judge, the height of the bench, or the voice of the doomster at least symbolize an established, legitimate structure of power.

Morton can scarcely be comfortable with the notion of right as Burley defines it for him—the mere trappings of existing power.[26] But Burley's charge leads Morton to question the authority assumed by the rebels in their acts of "punishment" more than to doubt his conservative tendencies. Unlike Burley, Morton can both grant the value of an act and deny the right of those who acted: "That the Almighty, in His mysterious providence, may bring a bloody man to an end deservedly bloody does not vindicate those who, without authority of any kind, take upon themselves to be the instruments of execution, and presume to call them the executors of divine vengeance" (chap. 21, p. 199). Without a firm sense of law, without a system of binding rules to guide action, Burley must inevitably return to irrational and personal grounds in defense of his right to punish. Scott makes it clear that Burley's appeals to providential signs, inspiration, or Scripture do not actually derive from an external, objective source. The Covenanter merely seeks from his own madness and his own ambition to claim the authority of a "mightier arm" that lends credit to deeds of violence.

This return to the language of the first discussion between Morton and Burley demonstrates the rebels' inability to provide an adequate alternative to the authority of the established government. The killing of Sharpe is no more an execution than the killing of Cornet Grahame, the bearer of a flag of truce to the rebel camp. The latter act, which shocks one of Burley's fellow officers, depends upon the same basis of right as the former: "Is it not written, Thou shalt be zealous even to slaying?" (chap. 16, p. 155). The terms of the debate between Morton and Burley remain fixed on such points throughout the novel. When Burley erects a gibbet for the captured Lord Evandale, Morton demands, "By what law can you justify the atrocity you would commit?" Burley's answer again rests upon a selective reading and understanding of Scripture (chap. 27, p. 251).

By such means Burley seeks the same assurance of power that Claverhouse holds so easily. As many readers have noted (and as Scott surely intended readers to note), the opposites mirror each other; Burley's exercise of power is no more arbitrary than that of his enemy. The royalist commander kills with less zeal perhaps, but with equal readiness.[27] Certainly the "drudgery" of dispatching rebel prisoners could elicit the same question Morton poses on Evandale's behalf (chap. 34, p. 308; chap. 36, p. 326).

His question cannot be satisfactorily answered by those who commit atrocities, but Morton at least lives to appreciate the answer history supplies: such actions as Burley and Claverhouse take are atrocities because they deny law. As Ferguson argues, the progress of civil society comes to make "government itself a subject of rules."[28] Niel Blane, the self-servingly neutral tavern owner, supplies the meaning of the revolution with respect to the right to punish: "There's ae gude thing o' the change—or the Revolution, as they ca' it—folks may speak out afore thae birkies now, and nae fear o' being hauled awa to the guard-house, or having the thumikins screwed on your finger-ends, just as I wad drive the screw through a cork" (chap. 41, p. 376).

Niel Blane's remark may remind us of the vivid scenes of torture that do precede the revolution. And these scenes remind us that Henry Morton shares with Waverley the disadvantages of a privileged position. At a crucial point in the novel he too is rewarded for his passivity. In an early study of the Waverley novels, J. L. Adolphus complained that Morton is left to look upon the torture of Macbriar with his "pardon in his hand." He is, Adolphus writes, a concerned yet "passive spectator."[29] Macbriar's fanaticism—even his earlier determination to take Morton's life—hardly eases the hero's awkward position. But, unlike Waverley, Morton shares the reader's discomfort. His passivity is barely maintained by a strong, practical necessity. Claverhouse calls Morton's attention to his situation, just as Morton prepares to act: "For God's sake, think where you are!" (chap. 36, p. 326).

Where Morton is, of course, is before the Scottish privy council in the year 1679. And that council's cool and ready willingness to punish with great severity makes Morton's rational attitude an anachronism of sorts. One hundred years later, Gilbert Stuart (like Ferguson a "philosophical" or "speculative" historian) could write of the rise of torture in barbarian societies and its continuance "to the disgrace of humanity" in the days of Queen Anne. This "odious prerogative," Stuart notes, "was adopted by the Privy-council of Scotland. And it is well known, that this . . . jurisdiction was to exceed the star-chamber of England in every thing that is most daringly and most exquisitely profligate."[30] But in the turmoil of 1679 the privy council was—however "profligate"—hardly extraordinary. We must remember the parade of severed hands and heads that Scott shows us moving through the streets of Edinburgh and leads future victims to the council's chambers (chap. 35, pp. 317–19). It is in this context that we may best appreciate Morton's rare qualities and excuse his momentary helplessness.

Stuart's humane wisdom (like Morton's) is a product, in his own terms, of an advanced state of society. In the more primitive, prerevolutionary condition of arbitrary law and violent response, of atrocity matched by atrocity, judicious mercy can gain little credit. Morton cannot save Macbriar from the savagery of the temporarily victorious government, just as Waverley cannot save Fergus from the consequences of Talbot's logic. Scott's uneven perspective on punishment in the earlier book, however, signals another important difference between *Waverley* and *Old Mortality*. Quite simply, at the time of Macbriar's trial our assent does not need to be given to the authorities; the equilibrium of the glorious revolution has not yet been achieved. Before 1688, Macbriar's suffering can enlist Morton's sympathy without compromising his allegiance (or the reader's) to the right political order. Rebellious feelings are condoned, even if rebellious actions are impractical. Character, author, and audience can share in a frustrated, impotent desire to help the victim. The lengthy anticlimactic resolution that follows the trial and torture scene in *Old Mortality* (a resolution that moves us ten years past the battle of Bothwell Bridge) may not be good reading, but it does allow Scott to avoid the kind of embarrassment he suffered in *Waverley*. By the end of *Old Mortality*, Morton can take his secure and rightful place in the postrevolutionary world without betraying those who suffered under prerevolutionary powers. Unlike Waverley, Morton has fought hard and suffered long for the position he finally achieves.

The shift in attitude that accompanies the progress of time is important, for it helps us clarify our perspective on the relevance of philosophical history to the practice of punishment. If in *Old Mortality* a humane attitude seems anachronistic amidst vengeful turmoil, the situation had been reversed in *Waverley*: torture is projected as the anachronism in postrevolutionary Great Britain—as an inappropriate, unnecessary, and wasteful expression of the sheer power of one group over another.[31] Indeed, such expressions were generally understood to endanger power by wasting it. It was partly for this reason that Scott feels called upon to apologize for the primitive aspect of Talbot's judgment in regard to the specific nature of Fergus's execution. Responsibility, it seems, is never more odious than when it demands that justice take shape in a prolonged spectacle. Even William Paley, who dispassionately considers torture's potential as an effective means to an end, betrays some uneasiness with the idea of torture. Apparently it is most defensible when best concealed:

> If a mode of execution could be devised, which would augment the horror of the punishment, without offending or impairing the public sensibility by cruel or unseemly exhibitions of death, it might add something to the efficacy of the example; and, by being reserved for a few atrocious crimes, might also enlarge the scale of punishment; an addition to which seems wanting. . . . Somewhat of the sort we have been describing, was the proposal, not long since suggested, of casting murderers into a den of wild beasts, where they would perish in a manner dreadful to the imagination, yet concealed from view.[32]

Such musings as these of Paley's were not widely creditable in the civil society of 1785. Despite the respect Paley commanded, he can hardly be considered representative on this matter. Torture had long been a rarity in Great Britain by the time of his *Moral and Political Philosophy*, and most writers of the later eighteenth century appreciated the "advanced" status of their era.[33] The sentiments of a pamphlet published in 1701 entitled *Hanging Not Punishment Enough* belonged to a distinctly earlier day. But neither the privy council nor its victim Macbriar are especially advanced. The clash between the primitive and the refined—so prominent in

Scott's work—does not arise in this instance from the relationship of punisher to punished, but from Morton's perspective on both. Ferguson takes a similarly superior perspective in his remarks on punishment in the "rude nations of America": "With terms of defiance, the victim, in those solemn trials [of torture], commonly excites the animosity of his tormentors, as well as his own; and whilst we suffer for human nature, under the effects of its errors, we must admire its force."[34] Morton certainly admires the force and notes the errors of Macbriar's nature: "'Marvellous firmness and gallantry!' said Morton, as he reflected upon Macbriar's conduct; 'what a pity it is that with such self-devotion and heroism should have been mingled the fiercer features of his sect!'" (chap. 36, p. 327).

The cruel Claverhouse, of course, reminds us that ferocity is much a part of the rebel's being. When Macbriar had Morton in his power, he considered the punishment of death a sign of favor, even a providential responsibility: "Then camest thou, delivered to us as it were by lot, that thou mightest sustain the punishment of one that hath wrought folly in Israel" (chap. 33, p. 303). Conversely, before those who pass the sentence of death on him, Macbriar uses his fate as a final demonstration of divinely inspired, heroic faith: "My lords, I thank you for the only favour I looked for, or would accept at your hands, namely, that you have sent the crushed and maimed carcass, which has this day sustained your cruelty, to this hasty end. It were indeed little to me whether I perish on the gallows or in the prison-house; but if death, following close on what I have this day suffered, had found me in my cell of darkness and bondage, many might have lost the sight how a Christian man can suffer in a good cause" (chap. 36, pp. 326–27). By placing Macbriar's two claims to authority in such ironic opposition, Scott strikes a balance he had failed to achieve in *Waverley*. Given the relative stability history brings, neither of Macbriar's claims threatens the world of his creator.

Scott has the diminishing figure of Morton recede into the future and leave the strife of 1679 in a vivid yet markedly distinct past. The separation, however, is not entirely clean—nor does the progress of civil society necessarily mean its unqualified improvement. An advanced, commercial society has its own liabilities. In the teasing final chapter of *Old Mortality* Scott intentionally deflates

our confidence in his authority as novelist.[35] Mrs. Buskbody demands—but he will not provide—a neat and happy close to the
tale. She presses for a static ideal rather like that which Scott
built for Waverley at Tully-Veolan. Peter Pattieson's comic, reluctant attempts to satisfy Mrs. Buskbody suggest that Morton
will inhabit no such place. The perspective Scott gains from his
place in history does not allow for an unmixed, confident attitude
toward the future. In fact, he can hold no such attitude toward
his own present. Postrevolutionary society is surely different from
and generally better than what went before, but it is also more
complex. As we shall see in *Rob Roy*, that complexity—apparent
in issues of justice and punishment—defies Mrs. Buskbody's great
expectations.

CHAPTER THREE

Rob Roy and the Business of Revenge

The state of high civilization to which we have arrived, is
perhaps scarcely a national blessing, since, while the *few* are
improved to the highest point, the *many* are in proportion
brutalized and degraded, and the same nation displays at the
same time the very highest and the very lowest state in which
the human race can exist in point of intellect.

—Scott, *Letters* (1829)

IN his sixth novel, *Rob Roy* (set in 1715), Scott seems to lead
well into a postrevolutionary world where memories of civil strife
are for the most part blurred by the comforts of a settled government. Entirely absent is the religious fanaticism of such men
as Burley and Macbriar or the royalist fervor of Claverhouse. In
the world of *Rob Roy*, Sir Hildebrand Osbaldistone—the hero's
hunting, drinking uncle—can hardly remember the consequences
of his past, dim commitment to the Stuart cause: "when his eldest
son, Archie, came to a bad end, in that unlucky affair of Sir John
Fenwick's, old Hildebrand used to hollor out his name as readily
as any of the remaining six, and then complain that he could not
recollect which of his sons had been hanged" (chap. 9, pp. 83–84).
The hero, Frank Osbaldistone, is even further removed from Jacobite passions; he wants nothing to do with any efforts to revive
the challenge to established government. Like the earlier heroes,
Waverley and Henry Morton, Frank is accused of high treason.
But unlike Waverley and very unlike Morton, he does nothing to
lend that accusation substance. Frank holds to his first position

throughout: "it is the most provoking thing on earth that every person will take it for granted that I am accessory to a crime which I despise and detest, and which would, moreover, deservedly forfeit my life to the laws of my country" (chap. 11, p. 103).

No one effectively contests Frank's assurance in the rightful power of the government. Counterassertions made in defiance of that power offer the hero no acceptable alternative to the status quo. Yet despite this presumption in favor of the established power, *Rob Roy* projects a deeply ambivalent attitude toward political and economic matters. This ambivalence seems rooted in the structure of the work. *Rob Roy* illustrates with special clarity a feature common to Scott's fiction: the genres of novel and romance seem somehow—much to the frustration of some readers—to contend for primacy.[1] But *Rob Roy*'s center of interest lies precisely in this unresolved tension between the novel of a young man's education in the practical and commercial affairs of life and the romance of that same young man's escape from the ordinary to a world at once more genteel and more romantic. This tension is significant in relation to large issues of genre and society. Michael McKeon has shown how the novel's coming-of-age involved neither a simple displacement of romance nor an "emplacement," or "progressive 'specification' of imaginative forms to the . . . circumstantial and material reality of human existence."[2] Taking off from the work of Mikhail Bakhtin, McKeon posits a historical theory of genre that dismisses the notion that categories such as romance and realism can be seen in opposition to each other. McKeon goes on to argue that the instability of generic categories cannot be isolated from the instability of social categories.[3] *Rob Roy* concretely illustrates the workings of McKeon's theory, for its mixture of genres or voices reflects what Scott himself would have considered an unsettling conjunction of two distinct historical stages.

In his 1829 introduction, Scott mediates (and in effect adds to) the voices in *Rob Roy* by explicitly pointing to the vital and arresting contrasts "betwixt the civilised and cultivated mode of life on the one side of the Highland line, and the wild and lawless adventures which were habitually undertaken and achieved by one who dwelt on the opposite side of that ideal boundary" (pp. vii–viii). Taking the perspective of a philosophical historian, he later suggests the value of those contrasts: the tale of Rob Roy's family

affords "an interesting chapter . . . on every stage of society in
which the people of a primitive and half-civilised tribe are brought
into close contact with a nation in which civilisation and polity has
[*sic*] attained a complete superiority" (p. xliii). Scott's juxtaposi-
tion of historical stages in the narrative reveals the liabilities of
the advanced, commercial state; it is a state, of course, that so
greatly rewarded and eventually bankrupted him.

Although *Rob Roy* never calls into question the rightfulness of
the power of king and parliament in early post-union Scotland (or
the Scotland of Scott's own day), it does reveal the individual's
vaguely felt or anxious connection to that power. A government
settled on the principles of the modern state, it seems, may achieve
its security at the cost of unsettling its citizens. Self-interest and
party spirit, old loyalties and new alliances—all confuse Frank's
ideal of peaceful citizenship. Frank abhors the thought of lawless
rebellion and asserts his innocence when any suspicion is raised
against him; yet he often feels like a condemned criminal, he is
protected by a notorious outlaw, he employs a horse thief, and he
marries the Catholic daughter of a zealous Jacobite. Most significantly, Frank's interest in the booming, mercantile world of the
early eighteenth century is secured by two acts of lawless, primitive revenge. First, Helen MacGregor orders the drowning of the
mercenary government agent Morris. Later (near the end of the
novel) Rob stabs to death the villainous turncoat Rashleigh.

Like the Waverley heroes before him, Frank must passively observe such horrors, but his position is complicated by the fact that
he profits directly and materially from the horrors he observes.
By these acts (both of which he earnestly repudiates), Frank is
delivered from the threat of false accusations, relieved of further
challenges to his rights of inheritance, and rewarded with the
woman he loves. To some extent, this complex mix of interests
underlies all of Scott's fiction; Judith Wilt observes that murder
and violence are behind the "stable nationhood that the Tory Scott
proposes as a frame for domestic-erotic security."[4] But Wilt's sug-
gestive lead takes a turn in *Rob Roy*, for authority in that novel
is not so much grounded in violence as it is preserved by it; despite the revolutionary tenor of the outlaw's rhetoric, Rob Roy
saves Frank's position in society. The good fortune Frank realizes
in part from the violence of others suggests, as Daniel Cottom ar-

gues, that justice does not necessarily advance with law, or even that law requires a restraint or formality that is not adequate to meet all conditions that arise in a modern society.[5]

Placed in context of the Scottish philosophical historians, Scott's complicated attitude toward social progress becomes more clear. In *An Essay on the History of Civil Society* (1767), Adam Ferguson maintained that the increasing prosperity of commercial pursuits may encourage an unhealthily focused, individualistic spirit: a sense of separateness replaces a sense of citizenry when the world of commerce becomes so complex that it demands and rewards highly specialized professional men.[6] But this corruption and decline of civil society is a possibility to be avoided—not a necessity to be lamented. Neither Ferguson nor Scott (at least not in his early novels) retreats into the past; rather, each uses the past to bear upon and measure the present. In *Rob Roy* the critical implications of this process are disturbing; primitive acts of revenge provide an unsettling parallel to sophisticated acts of business. Lawless revenge and lawful business (both of which reward and burden the hero of civil society) give rise to the historical tensions in *Rob Roy*. And together they obscure the relationship we often assume exists between law and justice, or illegality and injustice.

If business fosters an unhealthy independence, revenge requires it. As many Renaissance tragedies illustrate, revenge is an egotistic response to what is perceived as a private wrong. It presumes that law is too corrupt, weak, or clumsy to pay back evil. It replaces civil law with expressions of individual anger and thereby personalizes the meaning of pain for those who inflict pain. Finally, it is primitive in that it is lawless; it expresses a state of war. Hobbes makes explicit the dramatic point of the tragedies; he defines revenge as an act of hostility rather than an act of punishment: "neither private revenges, nor injuries of private men, can properly be stiled Punishment; because they proceed not from publique Authority."[7]

Rob Roy is no revenge tragedy, but—given Scott's great interest in and knowledge of Jacobean drama—a brief summary of such a work may provide a valuable insight.[8] At the end of Cyril Tourner's *Revenger's Tragedy*, Vendice—the only aggressively moral force in the play—is ordered to his death by Antonio for the revenge murder of the cruel and licentious duke. Antonio not only came to power through Vendice's actions, but has much reason to be satisfied with the justice Vendice exacted through the murder (Antonio's wife was raped by the son of the duke). Yet Antonio recognizes a threat to his newly acquired power in the moral presumption of Vendice. The new order of law and peace Antonio represents can allow no such ungoverned presumption.

Characters like Vendice, or Hieronimo from Kyd's *Spanish Tragedy,* or (less purely) Hamlet act in response to the past; they do not consider the meaning of their acts for the future—nor do they inherit the future. In this sense, they are (as Vendice realizes) their own enemies. Revengers pay off the past and leave others to possess the future. The Antonios of revenge tragedy are those others. They would understand Hobbes's rule of nature that in paying evil for evil "men look not at the greatness of the evil past, but at the greatness of the good to follow." Hobbes goes on to emphasize the practical necessity of this rule: "We are forbidden to inflict punishment with any other design, than for correction of the offender, or direction of others. . . . Besides, Revenge without respect to the Example, and profit to come, is a triumph, or glorying in the hurt of another, tending to no end; (for the End is always somewhat to come;) and glorying to no end is vain-glory, and contrary to reason; and to hurt without reason, tendeth to the introduction of Warre; which is against the Law of Nature; and is commonly stiled by the name of Cruelty."[9]

In *A Legend of Montrose* (a novel of the civil war, written in 1819, one year after *Rob Roy*), Scott depicts the political chaos that results from a revenge ethic. As in *Rob Roy,* the revengers are members of independent, primitive, and persecuted clans. They will not surrender their right to punish private affronts in exchange for public safety. This fierce tenacity eventually wrecks Montrose's hopes of forming an effective, lasting union of diverse northern clans against the parliamentary forces because it preempts any sense of shared laws or mutual benefits. It insists on looking backward. As Hegel argues, revenge, "because it is a positive action of a particular will, becomes a new transgression; as thus contradictory in character, it falls into an infinite progression and descends from one generation to another *ad infinitum.*"[10] Ranald MacEagh (the chief of an especially violent tribe) clearly

expresses the impossibility of escaping the past through revenge—
of finding an "end" to revenge: "Give us the huts ye have burned,
our children whom ye have murdered, our widows whom ye have
starved; collect from the gibbet and the pole the mangled carcasses
and the whitened skulls of our kinsmen; bid them live and bless us,
and we will be your vassals and brothers; till then, let death and
blood and mutual wrong draw a dark veil of division between us"
(*A Legend of Montrose*, chap. 13, p. 264). Such characters as
Ranald and his equally violent principal enemy, Allan M'Aulay,
cannot long submit to the discipline Montrose requires. They can
have no place in the coming complicated order of credit and co-
operation that is foreshadowed by the mercenary soldier Captain
Dugald Dalgetty and so fully realized in *Rob Roy*'s Nicol Jarvie.

In *Rob Roy*, Helen MacGregor makes plain the destructive
primitivism of revenge when she upbraids a servant who presumes
to defend Frank and Jarvie against her orders for their execution:
"Base dog, and son of a dog, do you dispute my commands? Should
I tell ye to cut out their tongues and put them in each other's
throats, to try which would there best knap Southron [speak like
an Englishman], or to tear out their hearts and put them into each
other's breasts, to see which would there best plot treason against
the MacGregor—and such things have been done of old in the
day of revenge, when our fathers had wrongs to redress—should
I command you to do this, would it be your part to dispute my
orders?" (chap. 31, p. 302). In this instance, Helen MacGregor aggressively invokes an "old" time "day of revenge" as a model of her
present authority. Like Ranald, she both perpetuates and accepts
the unending state of violence produced by a commitment to revenge. For both of these characters (as for the hero of revenge
tragedy) revenge becomes a consuming purpose of life.

Frank and Jarvie, of course, escape Helen MacGregor's fury,
but another of her prisoners is not so fortunate. Morris (a cowardly
agent for whatever side pays best) finds himself a hostage of no
worth. The government he serves places no value on his life. By
fixing a fee for his service, Morris becomes an item of use and is
treated as such. It turns out that his life cannot ensure the safety
of the captured Rob Roy. Once he has no value in trade, Morris
becomes an object of revenge. For Helen MacGregor, he represents a history of treachery against her people, a representative of

laws "from which they had often experienced severity, but never protection" (p. ix). The more Morris pleads for his life, the more he assures his death; Helen MacGregor will exact no less than the highest price she can from him: " 'I could have bid you live,' she said, 'had life been to you the same weary and wasting burden that it is to me—that it is to every noble and generous mind. But you—wretch! . . . you could enjoy yourself, like a butcher's dog in the shambles, battening on garbage, while the slaughter of the oldest and best went on around you! This enjoyment you shall not partake of; you shall die, base dog, and that before yon cloud has passed over the sun' " (chap. 31, p. 306).

Frank narrates the killing that follows this speech in a brisk, effectively dramatic fashion. David Brown finds the presentation morally ambiguous: Frank, after all, leaves it to the reader to decide whether to call those who dispatch Morris "murderers" or "executioners." [11] But surely Frank (and Scott) guide the reader's decision. Frank vainly attempts to speak in defense of the victim. He considers the killing a "horrid spectacle." And he records the agonized death-shriek of Morris heard over the wild, barbaric yell of "vindictive triumph" sent up by the Highlanders. In addition, the entire incident profoundly disturbs Frank: "[Morris] set up the most piercing and dreadful cries that fear ever uttered: I may well term them dreadful, for they haunted my sleep for years afterwards" (chap. 31, p. 306).

More compelling is Brown's assertion that civilized laws have little application in regard to Morris's guilt, for legal authorities sanction Morris's "crime." [12] If it is clear that Scott disapproves of Helen MacGregor's revenge, it is equally clear that he disapproves of Morris's self-serving, mercenary schemes. More politic and less passionate than his wife, Rob Roy (after escaping his captors) regrets Morris's death: "such a deed might make one forswear kin, clan, country, wife, and bairns!" But his regret is not long sustained by ethical considerations. Morris, after all, only suffers the death he intended for Rob, and "naebody will deny that Helen Mac-Gregor has deep wrongs to avenge" (chap. 34, p. 334). We need to ask how fully Scott implicates the government in his condemnation of the man it employs. Frank does not draw an explicit connection between the two, but his powerful and lasting response to Morris's death suggests some vague recognition that Morris's guilt is pecu-

liar to the advanced stage of civil society—a stage Frank seeks
to protect. This sense of a world at least partially shared by such
an unlikely pair as Morris and Frank is emphasized by the dying
man's last words: "O, Mr. Osbaldistone, save me! save me!" (chap.
31, p. 307).

Unfortunately for Morris, Frank can do no such thing. Morris
is efficiently and enthusiastically dispatched by the angry Highlanders in what Jane Millgate calls a "nightmare" parody of judicial
procedure, or a "mock-judicial slaughter."[13] The terms are well
chosen; in killing Morris, Helen MacGregor passes judgment on
the justice she has been subject to. And her act of violence gives
Frank reason to feel some guilt. Frank had—early in the novel—
teased Morris in mean playfulness and in turn been threatened
by Morris's false accusation. Those lies had never been absolutely
dismissed. Rob Roy warns Frank to stay clear of his two worst enemies: "[Rashleigh] has got the collector-creature Morris to bring
up a' the auld story again, and ye maun look for nae help frae me
here, as ye got at Justice Inglewood's" (chap. 25, p. 234). This conspiracy (as Rob Roy points out) puts the innocent Frank in more
danger from a magistrate than the guilty pair. Helen MacGregor's
cruel decisiveness, therefore, favors Frank as it strikes at the unwieldy machinery of the law he upholds. Somehow that machinery
obscures the truth of Frank's loyalty and blocks him even in his
thoroughly legal endeavors.

Nicol Jarvie provides some moral, civilized perspective on Helen
MacGregor's justice in his protest against the deed as a "bloody
and cruel murder," but the bailie's outrage is comically deflated by
his loquaciousness and his instinct for self-preservation. Frank's
thought that the bailie's "tone of firmness" probably impressed
Helen MacGregor must be understood as Scott's own irony. After
his initial protest against the act, Jarvie is made highly conscious
of his dangerous situation and willingly grants that concerning
the drowning of Morris, "least said is surest mended." Only when
Helen MacGregor forces him to a more positive answer does Jarvie
reluctantly repeat his first spontaneous protest, although this time
it is elaborately framed by pleas for mercy:

> "I see what you are driving me to the wa' about. But I'll tell you
> plain, kinswoman, I behoved just to speak according to my ain con-

science; and though your ain gudeman, that I wish had been here for
his own sake and mine, as well as the puir Hieland creature Dougal,
can tell ye that Nicol Jarvie can wink as hard at a friend's failings as
ony body, yet I'se tell ye, kinswoman, mine's ne'er be the tongue to
belie my thought; and sooner than say that yonder puir wretch was
lawfully slaughtered, I wad consent to be laid beside him—though
I think ye are the first Hieland woman wad mint sic a doom to her
husband's kinsman but four times removed." (Chap. 32, p. 309)[14]

It seems a dead wretch like Morris can inspire only a qualified defense from those who may follow him. As a man of business, Jarvie
understands the profit to be made in trade. If a word withheld or a
wink at a friend's failing can buy his personal safety, he is unlikely
to refuse the deal.

Despite his claims of kinship to the MacGregor clan, Jarvie—
a Glasgow merchant and magistrate—remains far removed from
the Highland world of his cousin. None of this is to deny that Jarvie
has his admirable moral scruples or his share of real courage. Nor
is self-preservation a characteristic peculiar to advanced civiliza-
tions. But the bailie is consciously attuned to his own interests
operating within a complex legal and economic network of individual enterprise. He, like Frank, uneasily shares in the world of
the executed man. It must be granted that Morris represents a
debasement and Jarvie an achievement of the commercial society
that Frank learns to appreciate. Still, none of these characters has
a profound emotional investment in the existing political estab-
lishment.[15] To some extent, all serve as employees rather than
devotees. The government cannot and need not command the kind
of obedience that clan leaders such as Fergus or Rob Roy inspire.

The debasement apparent in Morris's behavior is explicable by
reference to Ferguson's theory of history: in an advanced, commercial state a person can easily become a "solitary being"—detached from any felt connection with others. Because of the difficulties inherent in a primitive society, people there possess a
stronger sense of union; a personal rather than an abstract inter-
dependence undergirds the community. The attenuated nature of
relationships in modern society results in a justice dependent upon
legal limits rather than personal virtue or strength. Frank, for
example, seeks protection from the proper authorities partly because those authorities cannot overstep their call. They are bound

by specific laws and a relatively slow judicial process that guards against errors made readily and irremediably by those who act on primitive, lawless, or natural impulses. Ferguson also notes that the laws of civil society serve to "secure the estate, and the person of the subject."[16] Property figures as prominently as persons in shaping the ends of law. Legal limits, then, act as a conservative force.

Certainly it is easier for law to identify interests than to discover truth; but in the Waverley novels these two goals are not usually so ill aligned as they are in *Rob Roy*. Frank's persistent recourse to proper authority signifies his participation in and acceptance of the settled, post-union Hanoverian order. His trust in the protective value of a legal warrant, an officer of "competent" authority, or a man of high rank removes him from sympathy with the Highland law described by the bailie: "never another law hae they but the length o' their dirks: the broadsword's pursuer, or plaintiff, as you Englishers ca' it, and the target is defender; the stoutest head bears langest out—and there's a Hieland plea for ye" (chap. 26, p. 240). But such personalized justice has its advantages along with its dangers. Mr. Pleydell in *Guy Mannering* appreciates both. As an experienced and astute lawyer he helps Henry Bertrum retrieve his rightful estate, but he advises the farmer Dandie Dinmont to take up "good cudgels" in order to "settle" his dispute with a neighbor. Pleydell does hedge a bit when Dandie considers broadswords as a more decisive instrument, but the message is clear: Pleydell wants Dinmont to understand that law can be very unsatisfying for one who naively expects justice (*Guy Mannering*, chap. 36, p. 250).

Rob Roy, rather like Dinmont, can thrive without the limitations of formal laws. Scott's presentation of such characters suggests a position common among the philosophical historians. It is the very threat of broadswords—the potential abuses of personal power in a relatively lawless society—that makes individuals more conscious of their vulnerability and, therefore, of their mutual dependence. Without recourse to law, members of primitive societies are encouraged to rely more heavily upon personal qualities. Indeed, Scott's friendly enemy Francis Jeffrey (whom P. D. Garside calls "by far the most 'philosophical'" of the main writers for the *Edinburgh Review*)[17] cites the law's improvement as one of the principal causes of the declining character of the populace in nineteenth-century Great Britain:

> In the rude and primitive forms of society, when laws are few, feeble and inaccessible, men must depend, in a great measure, on their own efforts for the protection of their persons and property. They cannot go, at every moment, to swear the peace against a neighbour whom they have offended, or to obtain a search-warrant for the cattle they suspect to have been stolen;—they must protect their persons by resolute, but, at the same time, more courteous and circumspect manners,—by cautiously avoiding to give offence, which they know will be avenged,—and by maintaining such a carriage, as to deter others from offering any offence to them.[18]

In describing a nobility born of policy, Jeffrey anticipates Scott's characterization of Rob Roy. Neither Jeffrey nor Scott intends to idealize the past. Both make it clear that courage and courtesy are the best products of the rigors of primitive life, albeit not defining characteristics of that life. Helen MacGregor is a sufficient reminder of this qualification. Rob Roy's transformation from honest drover to rebellious outlaw, however, indicates no muddling of his historical identity. As a drover he was, Jarvie assures Frank, "baith civil and just in his dealings." And as a "levier of blackmail" he is "easy wi' a' body that will be easy wi' him" (chap. 26, pp. 243–45). Economic realities encourage the civil qualities (as well as the daring, adventurous ones) that characterize Rob Roy's dealings. Rob possesses courage *and* craft.

In his introduction, Scott unites the drover and the outlaw, the heroic figure and the scheming manager. He holds these images in balance by judging character (much as Jeffrey does) in the context of the lawless state that forms it: "as is common with barbarous chiefs, Rob Roy appears to have mixed his professions of principle with a large alloy of craft and dissimulation. . . . [T]he situation in which he was placed rendered him prudently averse to maintaining quarrels where nothing was to be had save blows, and where success would have raised up against him new and powerful enemies, in a country where revenge was still considered as a duty rather than a crime" (p. xxv). Perhaps it is this appreciation of self-interest shrewdly operating amidst difficult conditions that Scott refers to as the special province of Defoe (p. xl). Rob Roy commands personal passions in order to survive and even prosper without the sort of legal protection or recourse Frank takes for granted. In this respect, Rob is more like Colonel Jack or Moll Flanders than is his wife in that he can claim necessity to justify his outlawry.[19]

On the other side, Jeffrey's description of the corruption endemic to modern civilization suggests a host of Scott's petty, grasping villains who use law for an advantage they do not deserve and cannot justly earn. For them, law and business become indistinguishable. Clerk Jobson, for example, is characterized by Die Vernon as an entrepreneur of the law, who "finds it a good thing enough to retail justice at the sign of Squire Inglewood, and, as his emoluments depend on the quantity of business which he transacts, he hooks in his principal for a great deal more employment in the justice line than the honest squire had ever bargained for" (chap. 7, p. 66). Jobson is also, like Morris, a coward; law is both his protector and his abettor. For this reason, he neither attempts to avoid physical chastisement nor threatens to return it in kind; he anticipates profit from any unlawful aggression taken against himself. As Die explains to Frank, Jobson could live on "a single touch of your whip . . . for a term at least" (chap. 9, p. 87).

The sneaking, small-minded lawyer, of course, was an established literary type well before Jobson, but such weak and selfish characters observable in life cause Jeffrey to link the advancement of law to the potential debasement of men: "When a man can at all times enforce his claims by the sentence of a judge, and defend himself with the arm of a magistrate, it is no longer necessary for him to be either loved or feared as an individual; and, having no pressing occasion for the exercise of popular or formidable qualities, he is very apt to cease to be either brave or amiable, and to pursue his own sordid gains, or sensual gratifications, without regard to the opinion of his neighbours."[20] The impertinent Clerk Jobson, the disloyal business associate McVittie, the duplicitous agent Morris pursue their own gains without exercising "popular or formidable qualities." None are "brave" or "amiable." Significantly, all are defeated primarily by the justice enacted by the primitive Highlanders; the law of their own society plays a decidedly secondary role in purging itself of corrupt elements.

Nicol Jarvie, William Osbaldistone, and his faithful clerk Owen exhibit none of the profound moral decay apparent in the above group. But they do betray a crassness Jeffrey also lists as resulting from an advanced civilization: "Vulgarity is not the vice of uncivilized life,—but in comfortable trading towns, and cities of gay manufacturers."[21] Jarvie speculates on the profit to be had from draining a picturesque lake and using it for farmland (chap. 36, p. 359). William Osbaldistone's contempt for poetry in general is not redeemed by his contempt for Frank's poetry in particular (chap. 2, pp. 14–15). And Owen reduces the Golden Rule to an "arithmetical form": "Let A do to B as he would have B do to him; the product will give the rule of conduct required" (chap. 2, p. 11). It is this crassness or "vulgarity" that Frank first rebels against and never embraces. The lesson he supposes he has learned concerning obedience to his father is one few readers accept as central. The novel's end bears out the inadequacy of Frank's moral: he inherits the responsibilities of a country gentleman, not a city merchant.

That move from the countinghouse to the country house is finally accomplished for Frank by Rob Roy's killing of Rashleigh.[22] Once again Frank observes an act he cannot condone but cannot prevent—an act that terrifies him, yet rescues him. Again a lawless act of revenge prevents a legal injustice. And again Frank holds stubbornly to the side that has most often threatened him. His first act after Rob Roy's escape is to release Jobson from a dangerous situation and then enlist him as witness: "I . . . commanded him to observe that I had neither taken part in the rescue nor availed myself of it to make my escape, and enjoined him to go down to the Hall and call some of his party who had been left there to assist the wounded" (chap. 39, p. 392).

The wounded man in greatest need is the dying Rashleigh. Understandably, most readers have found Rashleigh an unsatisfying, clichéd villain—a demonic, crafty student of the Jesuits who needs no motivation to do evil. But Scott's hackneyed presentation should not obscure Rashleigh's ambition or the means he uses to achieve that ambition. Rashleigh plans to distress the Highland lairds who have done business with (and to some extent depend upon) "Osbaldistone and Tresham" by destroying the firm's credit. Rebellion is the goal of this mischief. As Jarvie explains to Frank, "the stopping of your father's house will hasten the outbreak tha's been sae lang biding us" (chap. 26, p. 247). It is hard to imagine the fate of Great Britain resting upon the fortunes of "Osbaldi-stone and Tresham"; but, however implausible, Scott's device is at least intelligible. The reader cannot miss the connection between business and politics. After all, Frank requires much patient in-struction on this point; he is not—to put it mildly—alert to the complexities of the family business. Indeed, when Frank demands an "accounting" of his father's property from his cousin, Rashleigh responds by accurately mocking Frank's previous lack of interest in matters of commerce. But Scott eventually rewards his hero for precisely this gentlemanly nonchalance. Frank remains at one re-move from the world of his father, and—by extension—from the world of Rashleigh as well.

Rashleigh senses opportunity in upheaval, but, unlike Jobson or Morris, he is motivated by more than material gain. In him the worst aspects of a sophisticated civil society—the self-centered, dangerous individualism, the lack of community, the sense of alien-ation—are complemented by similar qualities inherent in a primi-tive, revengeful order. Rashleigh wants Frank's money *and* his death. His language signals the complicity of his motives: "Do you think I have forgotten the evening at Osbaldistone Hall when you cheaply and with impunity played the bully at my expense? For that insult, never to be washed out but by blood! for the various times you have crossed my path, and always to my prejudice; for the persevering folly with which you seek to traverse schemes the importance of which you neither know nor are capable of es-timating—for all this, sir, you owe me a long account, for which there shall come an early day of reckoning" (chap. 25, p. 230). Rob Roy stops the duel that this speech incites, but Rashleigh's hatred is only intensified. After the rebellion fails, Rashleigh effec-tively continues his opposition by betraying his old associates and challenging Frank's inheritance. This stock melodramatic figure, then, takes on a peculiarly modern quality; Rashleigh finally be-longs with those characters whom Richard Weisberg has char-acterized as "ressentient" types—reactive individuals shaped by envy, "threatened by power but also bitterly seeking it." [23]

By legal maneuvers, Rashleigh nearly accomplishes all of his goals that had remained unrealized by theft and violence. But finally, Rashleigh is called to account for his actions by a more effectual person than Frank. Revenge is taken against Rashleigh, not by him. Rob Roy, the best representative of the virtues of a primitive society, foils Rashleigh's last plot and leaves him to a bitter death before his most hated enemy.[24] Rob does not then also die like a hero of revenge tragedy, but he does move offstage. His act of violence represents his final contact with Frank. He absents himself from the Lowlands and leaves the hero of civil society in safe possession of Osbaldistone Hall.

Frank's inheritance, however, is not illimitable; death marks a boundary to his happiness. *Rob Roy* closes on an unsettling note. The future offers no indefinite expanse. Although the entire novel is told by Frank in the first person, only on the last pages do we learn that he has both married Die and buried her. Frank is left an aged, childless widower. Alexander Welsh cites the impropriety of the marriage as the reason for Frank's fate—a fate unique among the heroes of the Waverley novels. Die is the dark heroine, a Catholic, a passionate Flora to Frank's passive Edward Waverley.[25] As convincing as Welsh is on this point, perhaps Frank's melancholy end does not arise solely from his choosing an unconventional mate. Frank's unwilling involvement in other improprieties suggests that gentlemanly qualities will not easily keep a place in the modern world. The wishes that prompt romance find only a partial expression in Frank's retreat to the quiet of his ancestral estate. That estate is tightly bound by the distressing concerns of history's progress. Although business helps Frank gain what is rightfully his, it seems an unsteady ally. Law also plays unevenly with right. And lawless violence on the part of others remains as much a part of Frank's success as any purchase or legal proceeding.

Scott's own life at the time of writing *Rob Roy* evidences reason for his disquietude over the sullied reality of certain emotional ideals. In 1816, Scott complained of "speculating farmers and landlords," and hoped that their economic suffering would "check that inordinate and unbecoming spirit of expence or rather extravagance which was poisoning all classes and bring us back to the sober virtues of our ancestors."[26] Yet a year later, Scott was busy buying up property and building onto Abbotsford. To be fair, Scott himself would not have considered these projects "speculative," but he was also at this time keenly negotiating over the terms of the publication of the sixth novel, *Rob Roy*.[27] Jane Millgate draws attention to Scott's use of anonymity in preserving these contrasting roles of gentleman and best-selling author:

> The Scott of the early Waverley years seems at times to resemble some hero of fairy-tale equipped with a magical power to generate wealth in illimitable amounts. But the new wealth had to be immediately transformed into something tangible that would not vanish— land, books for the library, trophies for the wall, all the furnishings of the second life that overlay the first and secret life. The special kind of excitement which secrecy created was enhanced by the sense of involvement in something forbidden or illicit—the comparison Scott himself invoked was coining.[28]

Millgate's reference to Scott's comparison is worth fuller notice. In a letter to the publisher John Ballantyne, Scott quickly moves from a self-satisfied thought on the purchase of some land to a faintly anxious remark on the means of that purchase: "I have closed with Usher for his beautiful patrimony which makes me a great laird. I am afraid the people will take me up for coining. Indeed these novels while their attractions last are something like it."[29] The date of this letter is October 11, 1817—less than three months before the publication of *Rob Roy*. Like Frank, Scott finds that his position depends upon support inimical to the quiet perpetuation of that position. As he makes clear in *The Bride of Lammermoor* (another novel involving revenge and inheritance) one may buy land, but not a "beautiful patrimony."

Scott's last words on the paradoxes of *Rob Roy* may be found on the title page of the book. Just before posting the first chapters, Scott sent Ballantyne a verse from Wordsworth's "Rob Roy's Grave":

> I beg pardon for neglecting the Announce. Remember that you copy it over. The first two chapters go to James today.
> Rob Roy in 3 Volumes
By the Author of Waverley etc etc
For why?—Because the good old rule
Sufficeth them the simple Plan

> That they should take who have the power
> And they should keep who can.[30]

"Taking" and "keeping" imply a more unsettled state of affairs than is usually found at the end of a Waverley novel. The former cancels the latter; the powers exercised on Frank's behalf corrupt the happiness that they grant.

CHAPTER FOUR

The Frustrations of Justice in *The Heart of Midlothian*

There is another and stronger reason still, why a criminal judge is a bad witness in favour of the Punishment of Death. He is a chief actor in the terrible drama of a trial, where the life or death of a fellow creature is at issue. No one who has seen such a trial can fail to know, or can ever forget, its intense interest. I care not how painful this interest is to the good, wise judge upon the bench. I admit . . . the judge's goodness and wisdom to the fullest extent. . . . I know the solemn pause before the verdict, the hush and stilling of the fever in the court. . . . I know the thrill that goes round when the black cap is put on. . . . I can imagine what the office of the judge costs in this execution of it; but I say that in these strong sensations he is lost, and is unable to abstract the penalty as a preventive or example, from an experience of it, and from associations surrounding it, which are and can be, only his, and his alone.

—Charles Dickens

IN *A View of Society in Europe* (1778), Gilbert Stuart argues that the "right" of revenge—though distinctly primitive and dangerous—cannot be wrested from the revenger without injustice; a modern system of laws, then, strives to civilize this right by depersonalizing it. Stuart places great faith in judges or magistrates who are supposed to sympathize with all concerned yet somehow retain the emotional distance necessary for making fair and effective decisions:

In the early ages of society, the individual depends for protection on himself. There is no tribunal to which he can appeal for redress.

He retaliates, with his own arm, the insult he has suffered; and, if he is unable, of himself, to complete his revenge, he engages his friends to assist him. . . . The most barbarous actions, and the most cruel disorder, are perpetuated and prevail. It is perceived, that the interest of the community is injured. Yet the right of revenge, so dangerous in the hand of the individual, cannot without injustice, be torn from him. It is equitable that he be satisfied for the wrongs he has endured; but it is no less equitable, that the public do not suffer by his violence. He is allowed, accordingly, to gratify his resentment, but through the power of the magistrate, who, while he feels for the injuries he has received, can also look with compassion to the criminal.[1]

The magistrate or judge, it seems, takes on the delicate, if not contrary, tasks of satisfying the wronged individual, protecting the public, and respecting the criminal—all while being an actor in a highly charged drama of life and death. Essentially laws and the individuals who carry them out must simultaneously acknowledge and domesticate the destructive tendencies of revenge. Only through such a balance, Stuart maintains, can justice (and society) be served. This legalized or controlled revenge gratifies the injured by an equitable return of pain. Such evenness or fairness in punishment administered by an involved yet objective party is the basis of Stuart's idea of justice, as well as the source of much imaginative straining; an abstract ideal (justice) depends it seems upon an idealized individual—a judge who is sympathetic and dispassionate, flexible and stern. Scott's novels make such individuals seem implausible at any responsible place in a system of justice: all act in the midst of feelings inspired, or of interests challenged, by crime and punishment.

In an earlier age, Stuart's desire to preserve revenge in the power of the magistrate could be justified in religious terms. Lord Stair, in his *Institutions of the Law of Scotland* (2d ed., 1693), argues that although punishment is not man's direct business, by "divine approbation" public authority must accept God's work and be (in Paul's words from Romans 13:3–4) "a terror to evil doers; and not to bear the sword in vain, for he is the minister of God, a revenger, to execute wrath upon him that doth evil." Stair goes on to explicate the passage: "By which it is clear, that the magistrate, as he executeth revenge, doth it not of or for himself, nor for, or from the people . . . but as he is the minister of God, he doth it for, and from God."[2] But the rationalist Stuart sees the magistrate's power as no more than a modern refinement of a natural, primitive, revengeful impulse. He does not possess Stair's faith, nor does he surmount the limitations of the prevailing utilitarianism of his own times. He considers revenge wrong when it upsets the community, but it is too satisfying a feeling to surrender altogether.

Stuart's blunt, commonsense habit of mind could not conceive of the alternatives Kant or Hegel were to offer in place of utilitarianism. Both emphatically oppose utilitarian justifications of punishment without supporting their opposition by reference to Scripture or to primitive, individual emotions. Both make a crucial distinction between revenge and retribution. And the latter concept means more than simply turning power over to the magistrate—more than civilizing what Bacon calls a "wild kind of justice."[3] Retribution is different in kind, not merely in degree, from revenge; a retributivist philosopher would insist that to redress wrong is not necessarily to revenge it.[4]

For Kant, punishment cannot justly be used as a means to any end other than itself; it is both right and necessary because illegal acts are wrong. Such benefits as the injured party's satisfaction or the prevention of crime are incidental matters. In cases involving murder, Kant argues that death is the only just punishment, for it is the only one that repays the deed in kind: the punishment balances the crime. Kant's antiutilitarianism is further apparent in his assertion that even if a civil society were to dissolve itself by consent of its citizens "the last murderer remaining in prison must first be executed, so that everyone will duly receive what his actions are worth and so that the bloodguilt thereof will not be fixed on the people because they failed to insist on carrying out the punishment."[5] For Hegel, the principle of retributive punishment is implicit in the criminal act, which "contains its negation in itself." Punishment is the manifestation of this negation. An abstract and displaced principle of right asserts itself against a crime in order to restore itself. Revenge for Hegel adds wrong to wrong; it does not justly punish by completing the criminal's "implicit will" as a rational being. This completion realized in retributive punishment rights wrong, a goal "which is the primary and fundamental attitude considering crime."[6]

Scott never formulates a justification of punishment as elaborate as Kant's or Hegel's, but he does demonstrate an intelligent and imaginative dissatisfaction with the limitations Stuart betrays. In *The Heart of Midlothian*, Scott (a secular-minded man of the Scottish enlightenment) asks if wrong can be redressed by an act of punishment that depends upon neither revenge nor utility for its justification. His answer is characteristically hesitant and indefinite; for Scott, human justice remains an imperfect matter of human laws subject, as such, to rational criticism and reform—but never free from the self-interest, passion, and uncertainty of the individuals involved. Acts of punishment, then, are never free from history, and neither is the moral evaluation of those acts in such things as novels.

Perhaps because of a tendency to seek in the heroine Jeanie Deans a clear guide through the moral problems raised by *The Heart of Midlothian*, many critics are led either to dismiss the novel or to construct unconvincingly neat resolutions.[7] Dorothy Van Ghent, for example, insists punishment has no meaning in the structure of the novel: it becomes merely "a kind of snuff to take away the odor of the offending deed."[8] On the other hand, Frances Clements sees the work as a coherent "dramatization of the theme of revenge, the harm it does, and the necessity for achieving some alternative mode of action." But for Clements, the alternative action is simple forgiveness, which still leaves punishment—as Van Ghent complains—a nonissue in other than providential terms: if we must forgive, we must not punish.[9] The long fourth and final volume does make providential punishment or fate an inescapable and perhaps ill-considered part of Scott's novel, but it does not cancel the substantial judicial issues he confronts in the first three volumes. In order to grant justice to *The Heart of Midlothian*, we need to appreciate the validity of the problems Scott poses and the difficulty of their resolution.

The difficulty is apparent in numerous attempts at defining the moral axis of the novel. Avrom Fleishman summarizes the central legal issues and concludes that "the novel is poised on the traditional distinction between a humane, commonsense justice traditionally linked with the divine realm (*la loi, das Recht*) and an institutional, historically evolved system of law which always falls short of the ideal (*la droit, das Gesetz*)."[10] But do we necessarily link either humane or commonsense justice with a divine order? Is "an eye for an eye" an expression of *das Recht* or *das Gesetz*? The

murder of Porteous is not humane, but it is more commonsensi-
cal than institutional. And, as A. O. J. Cockshut notes, the mob's
humane feelings regarding the hanging of the smuggler Wilson
fuel its brutal response to Porteous's reprieve.[11]

Punishment scenes in *The Heart of Midlothian* should be seen
as competing and inconclusive responses to a fundamental question: what kind of justice can punishment realize? The case of Effie
Deans (in which the government eventually forgoes the right to
punish) offers further insight into the sometimes necessary and
always uneasy linking of justice and punishment. For my purposes, this complex novel of the law and justice is about four executions—two legal and two illegal—and one pardon. Taken together
they constitute an impressive if only partial synthesis of the two
classically opposed justifications of punishment: deterrence and
retribution.

Scott takes us to the Grassmarket—the place of executions in
Edinburgh—immediately after his framing chapter involving the
two young and rather high-spirited lawyers Halkit and Hardie.
Peter Pattieson (one of Scott's several personas) meets these characters as a result of a coach accident that leaves them soaked and
stranded—a condition apparently conducive to telling long stories,
one of which provides the basis for *The Heart of Midlothian*. The
light tone of the lawyers' conversation serves as a starkly ironic
contrast to the gloomy setting that opens the narrative proper.[12]
And the layered introductions (Jedediah Cleishbotham precedes
Peter Pattieson and follows, in the final editions, Scott's own recounting of the Helen Walker story) provide by implication an
unsettling commentary on the nature of testimony and evidence.
To emphasize the point, Jedediah bitterly complains of those who
have questioned his honesty and the authenticity of his previous
historical narratives. His prolegomenon defends a past work (*Old
Mortality*) and prepares us for a new one.

The second chapter, however, wastes no time in establishing
the seriousness and the seeming authenticity of the story. Scott
describes the transformation of the Grassmarket from a fairly ordinary urban square into the sublime scene of death, and reflects
on its power to teach through terror.[13] The day is September 7,
1736—the day set for the execution of Captain John Porteous.

But before recounting Porteous's crime, Scott moves back a few months in order to make the captain's offense and the feelings it inspires intelligible.

The matter relevant to this purpose commences with the story of Andrew Wilson, a baker turned smuggler. Wilson's crime is not one to stir popular opinion against him. As Scott observes: "smuggling was almost universal in Scotland in the reigns of George I. and II.; for the people, unaccustomed to imposts, and regarding them as an unjust aggression upon their ancient liberties, made no scruple to elude them whenever it was possible to do so" (chap. 2, p. 19).[14] Although Wilson's trade is not generally looked upon as morally obnoxious, it is (from an economic standpoint) serious business to the authorities: smuggling "strikes at the root of legitimate government, by encroaching on its revenues, . . . injures the fair trader, and debauches the minds of those engaged in it" (chap. 2, pp. 18–19).

Because he is an active and daring smuggler, Wilson becomes a special target of the revenue officers, who eventually ruin him by successive seizures. Because of this "interference," Wilson considers himself the wronged party and responds by robbing public money from an officer of the customs. He and a young accomplice named George Robertson are arrested for the crime and condemned to hang. The sentence is justified on purely utilitarian grounds: "Many thought that, in consideration of the men's erroneous opinion of the nature of the action they had committed, justice might have been satisfied with a less forfeiture than that of two lives. On the other hand, from the audacity of the fact, a severe example was judged necessary; and such was the opinion of the government" (chap. 2, p. 20). This utilitarian justification, however, is exposed as incomplete on its own terms as the execution date draws near. We might remember at this point the common wisdom of Scott's day: the value of a punishment diminishes when it stands in contradiction to the feelings of the public.[15] After spoiling one escape attempt through his impetuousness, Wilson devotes himself to effecting Robertson's escape. In this he succeeds with the help of a crowd little inclined to assist the guards. His act of selfless defiance makes Wilson even more an object of popular sympathy, and the authorities grow to fear a disturbance or rescue at the place of his execution.

With Wilson's history established, Scott turns his attention to Porteous, a captain of the city guards, the man given the responsibility to prevent any mob action in Wilson's behalf. Porteous earned his commission as a reward for his "military skill" and "alert and resolute character as an officer of police." But he is also a "man of profligate habits, an unnatural son, and a brutal husband"—private qualities that make him both more formidable and less safe in his public position.

The dark side of Porteous's character is obviously important in respect to what follows Wilson's execution, but it is also important in examining the execution itself. What had started as a clearly utilitarian act becomes complicated by the feelings of the crowd on the one hand and the feelings of the executioner on the other. Porteous considers Wilson a personal enemy for his part in Robertson's escape. He is also annoyed by reports that the people may further dare to challenge his command by attempting to free Wilson. Finally, his pride suffers when the local magistrates request additional help from the militia in securing the peace on the day of Wilson's execution. All of these factors "increased his [Porteous's] indignation and his desire to be revenged on the unfortunate criminal Wilson, and all who favoured him" (chap. 3, p. 27).

Considering the detail that surrounds it, the act of execution itself receives strikingly little particular attention. Furthermore, Porteous—not the law—plays the central role in the execution. The law, in fact, does its work in a short paragraph: "Wilson himself seemed disposed to hasten over the space that divided time from eternity. The devotions proper and usual on such occasions were no sooner finished than he submitted to his fate, and the sentence of the law was fulfilled" (chap. 3, p. 29). Scott focuses greater attention outside of the strict dramatic routine that the law requires. Porteous acts with a severity beyond the role demanded of him. His conduct in securing Wilson against escape seems "truly diabolical." Manacles "might be justifiable" given the "bodily strength of the malefactor," but the handcuffs are found to be too small for Wilson: "Porteous proceeded *with his own hands*, and by great exertion of strength to force them till they clasped together, to the exquisite torture of the unhappy criminal" (chap. 3, p. 28; my emphasis).

Scott's attention to the government's intent, the crowd's response, and Porteous's behavior makes it clear that policy and passion can be at odds with each other. And neither has much to do with ideas of justice. Wilson's execution is not an "equitable" return in Stuart's sense; it offers the public none of the emotionally satisfying elements of his civilized revenge, nor does the state play its role dispassionately through an objective individual on behalf of the public. And surely Wilson's death does not fulfill the nature of his crime in Hegel's terms. On the contrary, its utilitarian intent debases the act. The government disregards Wilson's humanity by using his death to train other citizens in obedience. Such a calculating policy fails to credit a person's status as a rational being capable of appreciating the justice of an act of punishment.[16] Finally, Wilson's punishment serves no purpose outside itself; as I mentioned earlier, it fails on its own utilitarian terms. Rather than a "severe example" to those engaged in smuggling, it becomes a severe affront. Once again, Scott raises an issue familiar to legislators of his own time: justifications of punishment on the basis of utility are not complete if they fail to account for the public's response to the actual fact of punishment. As Foucault has pointed out—and as Scott surely understood—the message of punishment is difficult to control, and the difficulty can prove dangerous.[17]

The response to Wilson's hanging, of course, leads to Porteous's own crime. In the excitement that follows the execution, the captain exceeds the authority of his legal commission: "the sentence having been fully executed, it was his duty not to engage in hostilities with the misguided multitude, but to draw off his men as fast as possible" (chap. 3, p. 29). The amateur lawyer, Bartoline Saddletree, provides a comic twist to the significance of Porteous's belated actions. If Porteous had fired on the crowd *before* he hanged Wilson, Saddletree contends, no charge of murder could be filed. After the cutting down of the body, however, Porteous's task is complete. He had no more sentence to carry out, no more criminal to guard. One unsophisticated listener little appreciates the fineness of this legal distinction: " 'But, Mr. Saddletree,' said Plumdamas, 'do ye really think John Porteous's case wad hae been better if he had begun firing before ony stanes were flung at a'?' " Saddletree answers confidently, "Indeed do I, neighbor Plumdamas" (chap. 4, p. 39).

Perhaps surprisingly, Saddletree's confidence has some basis. If

Porteous's timing had been better, his legal case might well have been stronger (though his moral position would have been proportionally worse).[18] The criminal law depends upon fine distinctions: since crimes entail punishment, it is the law's task to define them with precision and prosecute them with consistency. Effie Deans's case nicely illustrates the weakness of this common proposition. In *On Crimes and Punishments*, Cesare Beccaria had argued that interpretation and obscurity were tools of repression;[19] but a precisionist view in Effie's case sanctions injustice with equal effectiveness. Indeed, it seems that inequitable punishment rather than consciously orchestrated repression is the more likely result of strict interpretation and enforcement; certainly the letter of the law—the thing Saddletree so zealously puts forward—is no less hard on poor Effie than it is on the cruel Porteous. This is not of course to say he is treated leniently: within the space of a page after executing Wilson, Porteous is on trial for murder. By the end of the chapter, the court passes the sentence of death upon him. In the minds of the populace, the sentence promises to revenge a number of acts: "the odium of *the whole transactions* of the fatal day attached to him [Porteous], *and to him alone*" (chap. 3, p. 29; my emphasis).

As the words quoted above suggest, Porteous's sentence (like Wilson's) signifies much more than his own guilt. The Scot's animosity toward the English and toward the Act of Union made Wilson a sort of popular hero. That same animosity makes Porteous's villainy all the more obnoxious to the crowd. He is hated as much for his legal role in Wilson's death as for his illegal conduct after the execution. Scott also suggests that class jealousies and interests increased "the odium against Porteous" (chap. 4, p. 34) and make truth a hopelessly problematic ideal.[20] I am not suggesting that Porteous's guilt is as slight as Wilson's, or that his punishment is comparably unfair, but we should remember that the crowd desires his punishment in payment for more than his crime. We should also remember that Scott's narrative makes Porteous's trial less than conclusive. The captain's guilt or innocence must be determined from a mass of conflicting eye-witness accounts. As readers we may be privileged with greater certainty than we would have as jurors. But even this may be doubtful; a legal, courtroom construction of an event seems rather like the historical, narrative reconstruction that Jedediah Cleishbotham (Scott's editorial persona) so fervently—and foolishly—defends in his prolegomenon to the novel.[21]

Whatever Porteous's just desert, the crowd finds it cannot trust to the law to complete its promise; Porteous gains a reprieve. The royal—and English—prerogative of mercy (which eventually saves Effie) here protects the unpopular captain, judged guilty and sentenced by an Edinburgh court of law.[22] The subsequent lynching of Porteous occupies notably more than the paragraph Scott allows for the hanging of Wilson. And the crowd possesses far greater composure in its act of "justice" than the officials who preside over Wilson's execution. Scott, in fact, wavers between the words "rioters" and "conspirators" in describing the crowd. Their claim is that the lynching respects both justice and law: "[Porteous] has been already judged and condemned by lawful authority. We are those whom Heaven, and our righteous anger, have stirred up to execute judgment, when a corrupt government would have protected a murderer" (chap. 7, p. 67). The crowd further asserts the rightness of its action by observing the niceties of a proper hanging. They provide a minister; they walk the victim to the place of public execution; they take care to show that "they meditated not the slightest wrong or infraction of law, excepting so far as Porteous himself was concerned" (chap. 7, p. 66).

George Robertson (Wilson's accomplice and, we learn later, Effie's lover) acts as the leader and spokesman for the conspirators. He first protects Porteous from the crowd's anger, for hurried savagery would not express justice: "would ye execute an act of justice as if it were a crime and a cruelty?" (chap. 7, p. 62). Such phrases as "act of justice" and "judgment of Heaven" set the crowd's stated motives sharply against the utilitarian goals stated in defense of Wilson's execution. Once again, however, motives are not as clear as the terms applied to them. Porteous carried out the law in a spirit of revenge; Robertson uses a claim to a more abstract justice in the same spirit. In addition, Robertson has an unspoken, practical end in mind: he wants to save Effie, who awaits trial on the charge of child murder. By leading the crowd to break into the prison to get Porteous, Robertson can break out other prisoners— including Effie. As for the crowd, Scott leaves little doubt that in spite of various claims of dispassionate justice, they want simple revenge. An ideal like retribution in punishment seems unavoidably spoiled by passions born of the extralegal forces of social and personal history. The crowd backs Robertson in his plea for an orderly execution, for like him, they are "desirous of colouring their cruel and revengeful action with a show of justice and moderation" (chap. 7, p. 62).

Scott feels the attraction of a justification for the act of punishment that is more right than useful and more disinterested than cruel, but he does not project this ideal in *The Heart of Midlothian*. To the frustration of critics like David Brown, who assume the crowd's action is just, the execution of Porteous is finally no more satisfying than that of Wilson.[23] Scott controls our response by refusing to flinch from an image of the crowd's revenge. We share the sight of Reuben Butler, the novel's hero and the unwilling minister to Porteous, as he flees the scene of the execution: "Butler . . . cast back a terrified glance, and by the red and dusky light of the torches he could discern a figure wavering and struggling as it hung suspended above the heads of the multitude, and could even observe men striking at it with their Lochaber axes and partizans. The sight was of a nature to double his horror and to add wings to his flight" (chap. 7, p. 67). The mob's anger finds its final expression in cruelty. Its orderly drama breaks down at the climactic moment of execution. Porteous is hurried to his death in a frenetic burst of activity. The horrible image of his final struggle defies the crowd's attempt to gain justice; a satisfying retributive act proves to be as elusive as a genuinely useful one.

Two other, similarly paired execution scenes occur in the novel's fourth and final book. These scenes have received very little comment; certainly they do not have the narrative significance or power of the earlier scenes. They take place as many readers begin to lose patience with Scott's lengthy conclusion. But they do provide a telling parallel to the execution/assassination of Wilson and Porteous. Meg Murdockson (the old woman who attended Effie in her labor) is executed by due process of law for "her active part" in an "atrocious robbery and murder" (chap. 50, p. 496). Meg's mad daughter, Madge Wildfire, is killed by a mob. The latter act is in part a result of the former. And any clear ideal of justice is once again lost amidst confused signals as to the motives behind the acts, or the consequences that follow such acts.

It is not immediately apparent who is being hanged in the first of these later scenes. Jeanie Deans, returning north by coach from her successful petition to the queen, notes a large crowd gathering just off the road near Carlisle. She and her traveling companions—two servants of the Duke of Argyle—learn that the activity is a result of the "laudable public desire 'to see a doomed Scotch witch and thief get half of her due upo' Haribee-broo' yonder, for she was only to be hanged; she should hae been boorned aloive, an'cheap on't'" (chap. 40, p. 412). Scott expresses scorn here for those who trust in the spectacle of punishment to express justice or achieve deterrence, although he had expressed a very different attitude earlier in the book (chap. 2, p. 20). Perhaps he assumes some crowds are more amenable to the moral lesson of capital punishment, but surely executions in this rude area of Great Britain seem merely a part of a general, brutal wildness. In such a primitive environment as Harabee, the spectacle of death can have little positive meaning. Indeed, distinctions between legal executions and lynchings seem vague at best.

It is not even clear to the onlookers at Meg's execution why she is being hanged. The crowd, for its part, considers witchcraft the principal crime; but witchcraft is not the offense (we learn later) charged against her by the law. Obviously deterrence cannot be claimed as a plausible justifying purpose if the viewers do not know what crime is being punished. Dolly Dutton, the dairymaid who accompanies Jeanie, is as unconcerned with the crime as the crowd is; she wants to see the punishment for its singularity: "I never seed a woman hanged in a' my life, and only four men, as made a goodly spectacle" (chap. 40, p. 412). Scott here nearly reduces the significance of the public show to a grimly comic level, as he does in an earlier comment offered through Mr. Saddletree: "I promised to ask a half playday to the schule, so that the bairns might gang and see the hanging, which canna but have a pleasing effect on their young minds, seeing there is no knowing what they may come to themselves" (chap. 27, pp. 278–79).

But the comedy does not prevail. Just as the hero, Reuben Butler, glimpses the mob's work, the heroine, Jeanie Deans, catches sight of the "terrible behests of the law." The two views, one of a lawless act of revenge, the other of a lawful killing, have strikingly similar effects on the main characters. We get our first picture of

Meg's execution through the rather dull senses of Dolly Dutton, who sees clearly

> the outline of the gallows-tree, relieved against the clear sky, the dark shade formed by the persons of the executioner and the criminal upon the light rounds of the tall aerial ladder, until one of the objects, launched into the air, gave unequivocal signs of mortal agony, though appearing in the distance not larger than a spider dependent at the extremity of his invisible thread, while the remaining form descended from its elevated situation, and regained with all speed an undistinguished place among the crowd. This termination of the tragic scene drew forth of course a squall from Mrs. Dutton, and Jeanie, with instinctive curiosity, turned her head in the same direction. (Chap. 40, pp. 412–13)

Jeanie is far more profoundly affected than Mrs. Dutton. It is not so much a shock to Jeanie's "nerves" as to her "mind and feelings." It is not then one that arises simply from associating her sister's recent escape from the gallows with the sight of Meg's lifeless form. Still that sight leaves her with a "sensation of sickness, of loathing, and of fainting."

Reuben Butler, of course, feels similar, even more lasting sensations as a result of his experience: "Butler, whose constitution was naturally feeble, did not soon recover from the fatigue of body and distress of mind which he had suffered in consequence of the tragical events with which our narrative commenced" (chap. 27, p. 274). The illegality of the act ("the peculiar and horrid circumstances") heightens Butler's response to Porteous's lynching, but his response is not primarily to the illegality. Nor does Butler doubt that Porteous is guilty or even that he may deserve death. The spectacle of death itself appalls him without regard to its sanction or its justice.

Certainly Jeanie's response is not softened by the knowledge that the execution she views is perfectly legal. Nor could she be comforted by knowing that Meg received an equitable return for her evil. But her revulsion indicates more than her deep human sympathy; it arises largely from an intensely inward morality that will not assess a public act without reference to private emotions. Jeanie does not place her own sense of right above the law, but she does seek desperately to make the two correspond. In effect, she feels degraded by a legal act of killing; she feels a public execution as a personal failure. This peculiar and difficult sense of responsibility first appears when Jeanie is given the power to save her sister by denouncing Robertson, who she learns is actually George Staunton, the son of a wealthy and respectable clergyman. She first thinks of this opportunity as "an act of just, and even providential retribution." But the sense of trading one life for another bothers her. In addition, she must "consider not only the general aspect of a proposed action, but its justness and fitness in relation to the actor." Robertson's crime, she decides, cannot be punished through an act of hers since it is a crime against the public but not against herself (chap. 25, p. 259).

If we take Jeanie's reasoning as representing Scott's final thought on the right to punish, we are left with very little punishment to concern ourselves with. Such a narrow and kindly definition as Jeanie offers of personal responsibility in public matters would (if generally accepted) effectively stall criminal proceedings. As I have noted, when forgiveness becomes one's responsibility toward crime, punishment is left to providence. But Scott uses more than providence; he makes it clear that Jeanie's own thoughts on such matters are, however noble, historically conditioned—at least in part the product of the "strict and severe tone of morality in which she was educated." Her greatness, as Georg Lukács claims, never overshadows her "narrow Puritan and Scottish traits."[24] Lukács's point needs to be remembered as a corrective to those who see Jeanie as resolving for Scott the book's many moral difficulties.

John P. Farrell, for example, in his ambitious study *Revolution as Tragedy*, sharply identifies the threat of the degradation of law into "an arbitrary expression of self-interest" as an important issue in *The Heart of Midlothian*, but goes on to argue that Jeanie intuitively understands that law is founded upon "the structure of social life."[25] But if this is so, then surely the individual has a responsibility to consider the "general aspect of a proposed action" even before the "justness and fitness in relation to the actor." The individual cannot simply forgive or disregard crimes that affect only others. Clearly, Jeanie's decision to keep silent concerning Robertson rests upon more than principle; she consciously iden-

tifies with those Scotch Presbyterians who she knows would consider it treason to pass on information concerning the killing of
Porteous:

> Jeanie felt conscious that, whoever should lodge information concern-
> ing that event [the killing of Porteous], and for whatsoever purpose it
> might be done, it would be considered as an act of treason against the
> independence of Scotland. With the fanaticism of the Scotch Pres-
> byterians there was always mingled a glow of national feeling, and
> Jeanie trembled at the idea of her name being handed down to pos-
> terity with that of the "fause Monteath," and one or two others,
> who, having deserted and betrayed the cause of their country, are
> damned to perpetual remembrance and execration among its peas-
> antry. (Chap. 34, pp. 259–60)

Such complicating factors by no means make Jeanie's principles
contemptible, but they do make apparent the fact that those principles cannot entirely overcome the moral problem Scott develops.

A final act of public violence ironically underscores Jeanie's
limits. Earlier she would not respond to Robertson's completed
and fatal act of leading a revengeful crowd; now she cannot respond to an impending act of a murderous mob. The former did not
seem to concern her directly; the latter interests her intensely. As
she speeds on her journey to the idyllic Roseneath, the spectators
returning from Meg's execution cross her path. They are torment-
ing Jeanie's old acquaintance Madge Wildfire. For her part, Madge
claims kinship with Jeanie—a far closer and more specific kinship
than Morris had claimed with Frank just before his execution:
"Eh, d'ye ken, Jeanie Deans, they hae hangit our mother?" Madge
grabs onto Jeanie's carriage and implores Jeanie's help, but the
mob—growing increasingly vicious—pulls her off. They take her
madness (along with their own bad luck with their crops) as proof
of her witchery (chap. 40, p. 415). Jeanie thus finds herself in a
situation common to Scott's heroes: she must helplessly look upon
an act of violence that could as easily be directed at herself.

Scott makes no definite connection between Jeanie's willful inaction concerning Robertson's guilt and her helpless passivity
regarding Madge's murder, but the threat of lawlessness that
Robertson represents should not be underestimated. Not only
does he lead the crowd against Porteous, but as Madge's seducer
he is largely responsible for her madness and her death. As Far-

rell puts it: "there is in him a willful criminality, the outward sign
of a personality in which the influence of positive and moral law
has been superseded by the influence of the will." And if Jeanie
refused to bring him to punishment, her author is not so merciful.
Robertson/Staunton's death at the hands of his unrecognized son
indicates "the virulence that Scott detected in Staunton's version
of revolt."[26]

The legal killing of Wilson and Meg and the illegal killing of Porteous and Madge make clear the extraordinary moral and practical
difficulties surrounding an act of punishment. In order to gain a
better perspective on these acts, we must consider the case of
Effie Deans, who escapes criminal punishment both in spite of
and through the law. Her trial and pardon constitute the novel's
central action. The law that demands her life spurs Robertson's
conspiracy against Porteous. And it motivates Jeanie's journey to
London in search of justice. It is a law born purely of policy—a
policy that rests upon no direct reference to the concrete facts of a
particular case. The government need not prove that Effie killed
her child, or even that the child is dead. Mr. and Mrs. Saddletree
spell out for us the law's practical appeal and its moral deficiency:

> "The case of Effie—or Euphemia—Deans," resumed Mr. Saddle-
> tree, "is one of those cases of murder presumptive, that is, a murder
> of the law's inferring or construction, being derived from certain
> *indicia* or grounds of suspicion."
> "So that," said the good woman, "unless puir Effie has communi-
> cated her situation, she'll be hanged by the neck, if the bairn was
> still-born, or if it be alive at this moment?"
> "Assuredly," said Saddletree, "it being a statute made by our sov-
> ereign Lord and Lady to prevent the horrid delict of bringing forth
> children in secret. The crime is rather a favourite of the law, this
> species of murther being one of its ain creation."
> "Then, if the law makes murders," said Mrs. Saddletree, "the law
> should be hanged for them; or if they wad hang a lawyer instead, the
> country wad find nae faut." (Chap. 5, pp. 48–49)

Saddletree's comments illustrate Alexander Welsh's apt remark
that the reality individuals confront in *The Heart of Midlothian*
is "undisguisedly a 'construction' of the law."[27] Effie's situation is
made more striking by the fact that the legal "construction" threat-

ening her proves false regarding her actions. She did not kill or
desert her child, but since no child is to be found the law presumes
the worst. The child-murder law in question was, for Scott, a bit of
history, but its logic possessed a more contemporary significance
in regard to capital law. Effie's case in some respects parallels that
argued against Lord George Gordon, the "instigator" of the anti-
Catholic riots in 1785. In defense of Gordon, Thomas Erskine re-
pudiated the charge of "constructive treason" lodged against him;
he should, Erskine argued, be judged "not by *inference* or proba-
bility, or, reasonable presumption, but . . . proveably." [28] Erskine,
whose speeches were first published in book form in 1810 and re-
viewed at length that same year in the *Edinburgh Review*, went
on to stress the importance of precedent in English law. Precedent
provides the concrete instance that protects against dangerous abstractions: "the law of England pays no respect to theories." And
later, "What does the immemorial custom of their fathers, and the
written law of this land, warrant them in demanding? nothing less,
in any case of blood, than the clearest and most unequivocal conviction of guilt." [29] Such evidence is precisely what the government
lacks in its case against Effie Deans.

Welsh also notes that Scott's romance supports or saves the law
despite the law's apparent arbitrary and tenuous quality. For my
purpose, however, the saving power of romance must be subordi-
nated to the common legal act it uses to save Effie. Largely because of the law's abstract severity, the royal prerogative of mercy
was often invoked—much to the displeasure of writers like Swift
or Fielding. [30] And the prerogative, as Leon Radzinowicz makes
clear, remained a point of controversy in the early nineteenth century. [31] Blackstone argues a standard line in defense of the king's
power to pardon: the role of the courts must be kept separate from
that of the crown. Judges and juries, he insists, are accountable
to the letter of the law. As Effie's judge puts it: "He and the jury
were sworn to judge according to the laws as they stood, not to
criticise, or to evade, or even to justify them" (chap. 23, p. 243).
But the prerogative, Blackstone goes on to maintain, provides a
human corrective to this necessary rigidity without corrupting the
law's literal content. [32] In effect, Blackstone replaces Stuart's faith
in the magistrate with faith in the crown. In both cases, someone

at a decisive point can be trusted to act with just severity and appropriate humanity.

Effie's judge, however, gives her little chance of escaping his strictness; despite his claim to the contrary, he does strive to justify the position he has taken and the action he anticipates. Past leniency has been blamed for present offenses; in order to prevent future crimes, the government chooses to be more harsh. Effie's situation is made even less hopeful by the Porteous murder, which personally offends Queen Caroline as an act of rebellion against royal authority; she has had, she says, enough of Scottish pardons. Jeanie's act of persistent faith in legal justice serves to challenge such discouraging circumstances. She quite dramatically forces the queen's attention to Effie's predicament. But Jeanie wins her sister's life by more than her perseverance or her eloquence. Queen Caroline arranges the pardon from a sense of policy as much as from a sense of justice. Her tactful fencing with the Duke of Argyle (who arranges Jeanie's interview) shows a queen alert to the advantages of occasionally placating enemies. Effie's pardon, then, is as much a matter of policy as the pardon granted Porteous. The king extended his favor to the captain as a symbol of support to others empowered to maintain the public peace. The public peace is much on the queen's mind as she uses her influence to please Argyle.[33]

Jeanie's speech then, as effective as it is, does not gain its effect wholly through its humane plea for mercy. It perhaps has a more powerful effect on readers of the novel than on Queen Caroline herself. Certainly Jeanie's simple humanity is sufficient argument to most readers as it concerns Effie, but it is Argyle who offers the most comprehensive dictum regarding punishment in the world of the novel. At one point he refers to the severe actions taken by the government against the whole population of Edinburgh for the affront of Porteous's lynching: "I might, indeed, be so unfortunate as to differ with his Majesty's advisers on the degree in which it was either just or polite to punish the innocent instead of the guilty." And shortly thereafter he moves from this general matter of public policy to the specific matter of Jeanie's concern. The queen complains of the mob's angry response to mercy in Porteous's case: "I suppose my Lord Duke would advise him [the king] to be guided by the votes of the rabble themselves who should be hanged and who spared?" And the duke answers by returning the issue to concerns of justice and policy: " 'No, madam,' said the Duke; 'but I would advise his Majesty to be guided by his own feelings, and those of his royal consort; and then, I am sure, *punishment will only attach itself to guilt, and even then with cautious reluctance*' " (chap. 37, pp. 389–90; my emphasis).

Argyle's advice suggests a morally pragmatic compromise between utilitarian and retributive justifications of punishment. In some respects, his position is similar to one taken by a modern writer on the problem of punishment. H. L. A. Hart maintains that the pervasive skepticism of our time has touched both of these opposed theories of punishment: "On the one hand, the old Benthamite confidence in fear of the penalties threatened by the law as a powerful deterrent, has waned with the growing realization that the part played by calculation of any sort of anti-social behavior has been exaggerated. On the other hand a cloud of doubt has settled over the keystone of 'retributive' theory. Its advocates can no longer speak with the old confidence that statements of the form 'this man who has broken the law could have kept it' had a univocal or agreed meaning." [34] It seems that for Scott the "old confidence" on either side of this issue never really existed. Argyle (or Scott) refuses, along with Hart, to provide a single justification for an act that encompasses "multiple issues which require separate consideration." [35]

Hart's terms may be set off against the duke's. Argyle insists on what Hart calls "retribution in distribution"; "punishment will only attach itself to guilt." But Argyle's sensitivity to matters of policy makes him a utilitarian as regards punishment's "general justifying aim"; the guilty may be punished, but only "with cautious reluctance." [36] Argyle's thoughtful balancing of justice with policy offers the most satisfying and realistic response to the complexities concerning punishment raised in the book. But it remains a compromise—an admission that the law's responsibility can be unpleasant, that valuable principles of utility and fairness can clash. To achieve a more unified response, Scott can only construct worlds more secure from the pressures of history. The ascendancy of romance or wish fulfillment over the ever-vexing frustrations of justice apparent in the early novels will be the subject of the following chapters.

CHAPTER FIVE

Ivanhoe and *The Talisman* as Romances of Justice

A judge to the accused: "Certainly you're entitled to justice, if you can show that you deserve it."
—caption from a *New Yorker* cartoon

IN *Discipline and Punish*, Michel Foucault traces the move from the body to the "soul" as the locus of the government's concern in its treatment of the criminal. Foucault interprets this shift as a means for government to widen its base of power. When punishment centers on the body of the criminal it can only operate within the physical limits of that body. As Fergus says to Waverley just before his execution: "Nature has her tortures as well as art, and how happy should we think the man who escapes from the throes of a mortal and painful disorder, in the space of a short half hour? And this matter, spin it out as they will, cannot last longer" (*Waverley*, chap. 69, p. 326). But the soul as the object of punishment imposes no such limits. Modern man discovers, Foucault asserts, the profit to be gained by extending punishment in time. Essentially reformation of the criminal laws widens and prolongs the government's power over its subjects; mere physical punishment concentrates power both in terms of who holds power and how the power is exercised.[1]

Foucault's main concern is with the motivating factors that underlie the reform movement and that continue to operate in determining our attitudes toward punishment. But in recognizing the complex self-interest that preserves and enlarges the prevailing system we should not underestimate the stubbornly enduring emotional appeal of older, more obviously brutal forms of punishment.

Such forms imply a longed-for (if not believed-in) unambiguous moral system—a system in which people get what they deserve. Surely Scott's exotic, medieval romances (as well as many current popular films and novels) glory in crude, physical expressions of power in which bad people suffer directly through the agency of the good or of God. Quite simply, doing justice defines just and unjust people; justice is not (as it usually is in the early Waverley novels) a frustrating matter of law and policy, but a dramatic revelation of personal qualities that make law and policy immaterial.

Of the Waverley novels, *Ivanhoe* (1820) and *The Talisman* (1825) best illustrate the attractiveness that wishful fictions possess as responses to complex problems. In these works, Scott generally replaces history with nostalgia; moral complexity with chivalric codes; and unsatisfying scenes of punishment with perfectly unqualified, swift, and certain acts of righteousness. The moral compromises offered by Argyle in defense of Effie Deans are made unnecessary by the conditions of romance, which make guilt and innocence easy matters to ascertain—punishment and pardon easy solutions to enact.

The nature and status of the exotic Waverley novels in relation to those of the relatively recent (especially Scottish) past has understandably been the subject of debate, for Scott's works aggressively mix what we commonly take as defining characteristics of genre.[2] For example, *Guy Mannering*—one of the more contemporary Scottish works—is in many respects a fairy tale of a lost child found; and *Quentin Durward*—an adventure of fifteenth-century France—provides a complex portrait of a scheming, politically astute, and decidedly unchivalric Louis XI. Nevertheless, it seems fair to say that despite the mixed nature of Scott's achievement, most readers intuitively classify the medieval novels as romances or even escapist fiction, somehow distinct from the prevailing realism of the other works.[3] In a contemporary review of *Ivanhoe*, Francis Jeffrey nicely set the tone of many responses to follow: "In comparing this work . . . with the former productions of the same master-hand, it is impossible not to feel that we are passing in a good degree from the reign of nature and reality, to that of finery and romance." More particularly, Jeffrey points out the indisputable fact that such a world as we are presented with in *Ivanhoe* could never have existed:

In a country beset with such worthies as Front-de-Boeuf, Malvoisin, and the rest, Isaac the Jew could neither have grown rich, nor lived to old age; and no Rebecca could either have acquired her delicacy, or preserved her honour. . . . Rotherwood must have been burned to the ground two or three times every year—and all the knights and thanes of the land been killed off nearly as often.—The thing, in short, when calmly considered, cannot be imagined to be a reality; and, after gazing for a while on the splendid pageant which it presents, and admiring the exaggerated beings who counterfeit, in their grand style, the passions and feelings of our poor human nature, we soon find that we must turn again to our Waverleys and Antiquaries and Old Mortalities, and become acquainted with our neighbours and ourselves, and our duties and dangers and true felicities, in the exquisite pictures which our author *there* exhibits of the follies we daily witness or display.[4]

It is important to emphasize here that Jeffrey's sense of the unreality of *Ivanhoe* as opposed to the realism of, say, *Old Mortality* arises not from matters of subject, structure, or even style, but from his recognition that goodness cannot provide an unfailing charm against substantial evils. Such charms do, of course, operate in romance, where (as Scott writes in his "Essay on Romance") the interest of the narrative turns "upon marvellous and uncommon incidents."[5] *Ivanhoe*, for example, ends happily thanks in the main to the extraordinary physical prowess of Richard Plantagenet, Robin Hood, and the hero. The equally extraordinary providence that kills the chief villain, Brian de Bois-Guilbert, and resuscitates Athelstane settles matters that remain. The narrative of *The Talisman* depends upon the astrological forecasts of the Hermit of Engaddi and Saladin's near-magical powers of healing and disguise. In contrast, Scott himself notes that the plot of *Old Mortality* turns upon the mundane clumsiness of Goose Gibbie at the wappenschaw.[6]

Numerous small incidents confirm the impression the tales of the distant past make as romances. In *Ivanhoe*, Robin Hood splits the arrow of a competitor who had struck the target's center; and this feat is only a prelude to more impressive marksmanship. Even Henry Morton's dexterity in hitting the popinjay from a galloping horse pales by comparison. The difference here is crucial. The picture of Morton that emerges from the wappenschaw is one of a young man imperfectly aware of his own potential. We are prepared to appreciate the influence of chance circumstances that make him into an uncomfortable hero of moderation. Robin Hood's character and role, however, emerge complete in his initial, sassy display of physical virtuosity: the outlaw's superiority to the tests arranged by the evil Prince John clearly defines and fixes his place on the side of a goodness that cannot be defeated. Morton's character, then, is imagined as operating within a complicated and realistic set of conditions (Morton's horse was well trained for the deed, he could have missed, etc.), whereas Robin Hood serves as an emblem in a purposefully simplified moral world. Of course Robin Hood is a relatively minor character in *Ivanhoe*, but the correspondence of physical strength, skill, and victory with virtue and right works consistently either for or against all the characters in the medieval romances.

Jeffrey is not the only critic to note the extraordinarily unrealistic faith the medieval romances communicate in linking athletic accomplishments with justice.[7] In his general essay on the Waverley novels, first published in 1858, Walter Bagehot explains the popularity of *Ivanhoe* by referring to precisely this faith: "The charm of *Ivanhoe* is addressed to a simpler sort of imagination—to that kind of boyish fancy which idolizes medieval society as the 'fighting time.' Every boy has heard of tournaments, and has a firm persuasion that in an age of tournaments life was thoroughly well understood."[8] Such a boyish understanding makes justice a simple matter of winning or losing. In this respect a tournament is a kind of trial by combat: both determine as well as punish guilt. Judgment and justice are dramatically realized in a single, trusty act of competitive violence. Alice Chandler echoes Bagehot's insight by stressing the longing for justice as central to the appeal of the medieval works: "The medieval novels enhance the world they depict. Despite certain tensional ironies and contradictions, they appeal not only to the reader's desire for heroic action but to his idealized conceptions of nobility and justice."[9]

Chandler's emphasis on Scott's brand of nostalgic medievalism has been the subject of some informed criticism by P. D. Garside, and Judith Wilt has made a provocative case for the centrality of *Ivanhoe* in the Scott canon; but *Ivanhoe* and *The Talisman* at least support Chandler's reading of these works as romances—as nostalgic dreams of order rather than forays into the nightmare of history.[10] The idealization of justice that Chandler calls attention to is most apparent in scenes of physical confrontation. In *Ivanhoe* contests or tournaments invariably prove accurate indicators of moral right. Ivanhoe, fighting incognito as the "Disinherited Knight," defeats five champions of foreign tyranny at Prince John's gathering. The next day he wins (with the help of the disguised King Richard) despite serious injuries and against long odds in the general melee. The woodsman Locksley (i.e., Robin Hood) triumphs dramatically at the archery competition. And, of course, Brian de Bois-Guilbert is done in by the force of his own passions as he charges toward a seemingly defenseless Ivanhoe, who champions the unjustly accused Rebecca. This conception of justice by combat serves no less effectively in more minor disputes. The swineherd Gurth defends his honor and his master's pocketbook in a lower-class contest with an underling of Robin Hood's band. And Richard proves his mettle in a good-spirited (but still morally and socially informative) exchange of blows with Friar Tuck.

Despite Saladin's prudent refusal to battle Richard at the close of *The Talisman*, "fighting time" seems still in effect in the later romance.[11] Sir Kenneth and Saladin—the two best representatives of their respective cultures' virtues—fight to a bloodless draw in the book's opening scene; each, however, wins the other's (and the reader's) admiration by fighting well and fairly. Toward the end of the book, Sir Kenneth defeats the traitor Conrad in a joust that both settles the mystery of the stolen standard and punishes the culprit. Conrad obviously feels the justice realized by the injury to his body as he confesses his crime to the triumphant party.

The scene of Conrad's defeat deserves close attention, for it so precisely illustrates the idealized benefits of public, physical punishment. Judicial combat (like judicial torture) reveals truth; not only does Conrad become what Foucault would call "the herald of his own condemnation," but he indicates that he is not alone in his treason. Furthermore, judicial combat establishes a clear connection between the crime and its punishment. And this connection is dramatically clear "because it occurs exactly at the juncture between the judgment of men and the judgment of God."[12] Scott's treatment requires quotation in full:

> The victory was not in doubt—no, not one moment. . . . Sir Kenneth's lance had pierced through a shield, through a plated corselet of

Milan steel, through a "secret," or a coat of linked mail, worn beneath the corselet, had wounded him deep in the bosom, and borne
him from the saddle, leaving the truncheon of the lance fixed in the
wound. The sponsors, heralds, and Saladin himself, descending from
his throne, crowded around the wounded man; while Sir Kenneth,
who had drawn his sword ere yet he discovered his antagonist was
totally helpless, now commanded him to avow his guilt. The helmet
was hastily unclosed, and the wounded man, gazing wildly on the
skies, replied—"What would you more? God hath decided justly: I
am guilty; but there are worse traitors in the camp than I. In pity to
my soul, let me have a confessor!" (Chap. 28, p. 302)

The passage is extraordinary; it is as if Sir Kenneth's lance, by
piercing through layer upon layer of Conrad's armor, finds not only
the villain's bosom but also the very heart of truth and justice.

We need no reference to Foucault to enlarge upon the virtues
evident in Conrad's trial and punishment. Beccaria, Fielding,
Blackstone, and Bentham all stress the usefulness of promptly following judgment with punishment.[13] Only by such proximity can
crime and punishment be effectively linked in the understanding of
the criminal and in that of the public. The power of punishment's effect, then, depends largely on the nearness of the perceived cause.
In *The Talisman* the relationship of cause and effect could not
be more compressed. Conrad's trial, conviction, and punishment
are all expressed by the forceful and accurate strike of Kenneth's
lance, which penetrates through deception, determines guilt, and
administers pain.

Nearly all the characters in *The Talisman* trust in some alliance of victory and virtue. Only the Templar, who does not believe
in virtue, flatly denies this alliance. Conversely, it is a mark of
Edith's purity that she never worries over her lover's success in
battle; she has illimitable faith in the trial by combat as "an appeal
to the justice of God." We should note the similarity between the
weakened Ivanhoe's courage in facing Bois-Guilbert and Edith's
brave pronouncement: "[Conrad] is guilty. . . . I myself, in such
a cause, would encounter him without fear" (chap. 27, p. 295). For
his part, Conrad's small portion of good nature (he is not, as he
says, "the worst traitor in camp") makes him a beaten man before the actual fight. No doubt if Edith could have challenged him,
Conrad would have accommodated justice (as Bois-Guilbert does

in *Ivanhoe*) by suffering a stroke. His lack of confidence stems from the recognition that if wrong is to be proved, it must be upon his body—not that of a noble opponent. And it is clear that his failure is not simply one of courage. He strikes Sir Kenneth a "knightly blow and true," but the blow does not carry the necessary moral weight to unhorse the hero.

All of this seems far from the Scott of *The Heart of Midlothian*. Physical strength in that novel suggests danger, for it tempts the possessor to engage in destructive, antisocial acts. Reuben Butler could hardly be a champion of right against the vigorous Robertson; neither Butler's society nor his health would allow him to take such a role. Fortunately for him, modern law and order rests upon different ground. As Scott points out in his "Essay on Chivalry" (first published in 1818, the same year as *The Heart of Midlothian*), trying "doubtful cases by the body of a man" is likely to be both inconvenient and unjust.[14] Although Scott does grant that the manners of the chivalric age possessed a "grace and dignity unknown to classic times," and that the "unsettled and misruled state of things" prevalent in the Middle Ages gave individuals a wider latitude in righting wrongs by force, he also points to various cheats or corruptions often practiced on the field of honor. Strength and purity are not necessarily allied in any stage of actual civil society; bullies and tricksters often defeat worthy foes.[15] But *Ivanhoe* and *The Talisman* present no such unromantic failures of chivalric ideals. Despite Scott's introductory disavowal in *Ivanhoe* of the "dangerous and fatal doctrine" of virtue's natural material reward (that is, the Jewish Rebecca cannot marry the Saxon hero), he does give virtue the stronger arms, the swifter horses, and ultimately the better luck.

The wishful ideal of justice also appears in the at least half-conscious willingness of many characters to accept punishment or the rightness of their defeat. As I have noted, Bois-Guilbert's heart bursts before he can consummate the evil his brain imagines. And Conrad not only admits his guilt but also grants the justness of the pain he suffers for that guilt. This willingness is, however, most telling in those characters least deserving of punishment. We might remember that in *Rob Roy*, Frank proclaims an abstract willingness to suffer for the crimes he is charged with; the feeling is merely potential, however, because Frank assumes guilt as a condition for its existence. But the virtuous characters of Scott's exotic novels require no such condition for their surrender; their sense of obedience makes the claim of innocence irrelevant since it preempts any selfish instinct—even in matters of life and death.

One variation of this tendency to embrace punishment occurs at the center of *Ivanhoe*. Authority, it seems, sustains itself by the obedience it inspires. The jester Wamba, disguised as a friar, offers to trade places (and thereby die for) his imprisoned master, Cedric. Cedric, in turn, will only accept Wamba's robes if he can then pass them on to Athelstane. Athelstane refuses the arrangement. Cedric is finally persuaded to escape in order to help save the others. Each aspires to the strangely enviable role Sydney Carton will play in *A Tale of Two Cities*. Like Carton, none of these characters is guilty of any crime; they are threatened by lawless Normans. The word "punishment," therefore, does not strictly apply here. But the Saxons are all willing to die to preserve the ideal relations that bind them in life. Wamba's request to Cedric emphasizes the moral: "let my cockscomb hang in the hall at Rotherwood, in memory that I flung away my life for my master, like a faithful—fool" (chap. 26, p. 234). From the individual's selfish point of view, relinquishing life must seem foolish, but faith in existing social relations overcomes the common wisdom of self-preservation.

The willingness of virtuous characters to die by the hand of another is more relevant to my interests when that other represents a rightful and unchallenged power. Submission then implies not so much faith in social relations as acceptance of established political authorities. I noted in chapter 1 that Waverley could take no comfort in William Paley's selfless ideal of the innocent, heroically passive sufferer who submits to death in deference to the settled order. But the most noble characters in *The Talisman* do not possess even Waverley's instinct for survival; when deemed guilty by an acknowledged figure of authority they are the most passive of passive heroes. Even the dark hero, Saladin, disguised as the physician El Hakim, does not hesitate to offer his services to the ailing King Richard despite the terms of "hard justice" offered him: "If I fail, ye wear swords thirsting for the blood of the faithful, and I proffer my body to your weapons" (chap. 9, pp. 102–3). If the Saracen willingly accepts such terms from his enemies, it should not be surprising that Sir Kenneth does not wait to accept equally hard terms from his master—he volunteers such terms himself. King Richard asks if the Scottish Knight will take the responsibility of protecting England's banner: " 'Willingly,' said Kenneth; 'and will discharge it upon penalty of my head' " (chap. 11, p. 131).

Sir Kenneth is altogether earnest in his promise. When he is tricked into leaving his post and thereby loses the banner, he repeatedly resigns himself—without dispute or qualification—to the terms of his contract, even though the Hakim points out to him that passivity in such a case constitutes suicide. Kenneth resists such a notion with the force gained from an even stronger prohibition: " 'God forbid!' replied the Scot, crossing himself; 'but we are also forbidden to avoid the punishment which our crimes have deserved' " (chap. 14, p. 155). Facing the prospect of immediate death, Kenneth stands "as firm as a marble statue . . . within the due reach for a blow" from the king's unsheathed sword. He sincerely considers the king "kind" for then ordering a simple beheading and foregoing the ritual mutilation of the body. He stoically accepts what seems the final, considered decision of Richard; when asked to prepare for "instant death," Kenneth "patiently" responds: "God's pleasure and the King's be done. . . . I neither contest the justice of the sentence nor desire delay of the execution" (chap. 15, pp. 159–63). And lastly, he refuses the help of the king's friend and adviser, DeVaux, who hopes to put a favorable construction on Sir Kenneth's failure. The Scot will not cooperate with those who would defend him: "I have deserted my charge— the banner intrusted to me is lost. When the headsman and block are prepared, the head and trunk are ready to part company" (chap. 15, p. 164). Sir Kenneth's behavior indicates that everything is clear, even to the one who will suffer justice.

Edith shares her lover's preference for uncomplicated and definitive judicial decisions, despite the risk of their severity. Although she pleads for Sir Kenneth's life, she does not do so on the basis of mercy but of justice; she is no Portia who humanizes the law by the ironic means of its own technical fineness. Edith not only seeks Sir Kenneth's life but also strives for absolution of any wrongdoing. He was, after all, tricked away from one duty by a charade of another. The queen herself made it seem that Edith had summoned Sir Kenneth from his post. Kenneth, therefore, merely obeyed a prior allegiance at the expense of an immediate one. If Richard cannot accept her argument, Edith contends, he should not qualify his anger. Her sense of justice is not assuaged by Richard's reluctant decision to give Kenneth to El Hakim in repayment of the physician's services: " 'Plantagenet,' said Edith, 'should have either pardoned an offense or punished it. . . . To have doomed the unfortunate to death might have been severity, but had a show of justice!' " (chap. 20, p. 209).

The principles of the two lovers are far less humanely flexible than those Francis Hart finds characteristic of the Waverley novels.[16] But the severe fiction of the subject's willingness to die by order of the state is not peculiar to Scott's romances. In capital cases, the criminal's confession is traditionally valued because it sanctions the state's fury. Sir Kenneth's eagerness to die, then, may be best understood in context of numerous other responses to those who in Scott's time contested the final extension of the power to punish. Beccaria had challenged the right of the state to take life on the grounds that the social contract cannot include an individual's promise to surrender life. The sovereignty of the laws derive from the general will, or "the aggregate of particular wills." None of those particular wills can rightfully subject itself to death: "Was there ever a man who can have wished to leave to other men the choice of killing him? Is it conceivable that the least sacrifice of each person's liberty should include sacrifice of the greatest of all goods, life? And if that were the case, how could such a principle be reconciled with the other, that man is not entitled to take his own life? He must be, if he can surrender that right to others or to society as a whole."[17]

In equating the principle of the state's right to kill wrongdoers with that of the individual's right to suicide, Beccaria reminds us of El Hakim's plea to Kenneth: by staying to "certain destruction" the knight is, in effect, killing himself. In resisting that argument, Kenneth becomes a figure much like one commonly proffered by defenders of capital punishment as an implicit response to Beccaria: the figure of the condemned subject supposedly eager to repay society on the gallows.

Such a figure peacefully resigned to the state's judgment had long been a staple of the most vulgar popular literature, but Scott was not the only (or the most) respectable literary man to indulge in this fiction. Wordsworth's "Sonnets on Punishment by Death" somberly articulate the virtues of the condemned's self-abnegation. This sonnet series addresses efforts (in the late 1830s) to end all capital punishments.[18] First published in *The Quarterly Review* (1841), Wordsworth's sonnets assert that duty may calm and guide the death-welcoming criminal:

> And some, we know, when they by wilful act
> A single human life have wrongly taken,
> Pass sentence on themselves, confess the fact,
> And to atone for it, with soul unshaken
> Kneel at the feet of Justice, and for faith
> Broken with all mankind solicit Death.

Later in the sequence, Wordsworth further idealizes the willing victim as a "kneeling penitent," softened by remorseful feelings stirred by his impending doom—a doom that it would be both unkind and unwise to delay:

> Welcome, death! while Heaven
> Does in this change exceedingly rejoice;
> While yet the solemn heed the State hath given
> Helps him to meet the last tribunal's voice
> In faith, which fresh offences, were he cast
> On old temptations, might for ever blast.

Beccaria was answered more directly, in less purely fictional terms, by other writers on law and punishment. A practical objection to Beccaria's logic was that it could be extended to all punishments and thereby undermine society; could a person surrender to prison or humiliation any more than to death on the basis of a prior contract?[19] Hegel denied the validity of Beccaria's contract theory of the state altogether; he maintained that since an injury possesses a "positive existence" in the "particular will of the criminal," that will must be annulled by an injury equal in value. Considerations of justice are of a higher nature than those of the state, and only in such terms is the criminal treated like a rational being—"not as a harmful animal who has to be made harmless, or with a view to deterring and reforming him."[20] Kant does not attack the social contract idea itself, but he does reject Beccaria's use of that idea. He argues that one cannot choose to be punished because punishment must be exacted by an objective power: "The social contract does not include the promise to permit oneself to be punished and thus to dispose of oneself and of one's life, because, if the only ground that authorizes the punishment of an evildoer were a promise that expresses his willingness to be punished, then it would be left up to him to find himself liable to punishment, and the criminal would be his own judge." [21]

The controversy that Beccaria raised over the individual's consent to the state's right to take life was anticipated by Hobbes, who distinguished between two promises: (1) "Unless I do so, or so, kill me"; (2) "Unless I do so, or so, I will not resist you when you come to kill me." Hobbes considers it impossible to make the second promise; the first, however, is a different matter, for it acknowledges the necessary fact of power without having the individual surrender the basic right of self-preservation. [22] Quite simply, the state cannot expect the criminal to welcome punishment; nevertheless, it can rightfully drag the criminal to the gallows. But Beccaria's sensitivity to the potential abuse of power made the first promise an unthinkable alternative to what he would agree was the impossibility of the second: once the state's right to kill supersedes the individual's right to life, any residue of self-preservation becomes insignificant. Scott's medieval heroes usually defuse the debate, for they accept so one-sided a social contract. Sir Kenneth's behavior (like Wordsworth's guilty man or Paley's innocent but convicted man) indicates that for him the first promise ("Unless I do so, or so, kill me") equals the second ("Unless I do so, or so, I will not resist when you come to kill me"); he empowers the state through his total personal submission.

To some extent, the innocent (or at least good) man's willingness to die for others, for honor, or for reverence of the state's authority (another theme of Wordsworth and Paley) becomes a moot point in Scott's romances. The very fact that such characters express an exalted commitment to ideals of loyalty, honor, and truth protects them from suffering on behalf of this commitment; there are only would-be martyrs in *Ivanhoe* and *The Talisman*. Wamba, Cedric, and Athelstane are all rescued from the lawless Normans. El Hakim ensures his safety by curing Richard. Sir Kenneth regains and even enlarges his reputation. All resignedly face death by the hand of others; none succumbs to that death. If the mortal suffering of Bois-Guilbert or Conrad proves guilt, the worldly salvation of the others indicates right and innocence (that is, after the proper gestures to authority have been made).

For example, Ivanhoe's famous last-minute rescue of Rebecca effectively invalidates the false judgment of witchcraft made against her by the Templar's ecclesiastical court. A just outrage against that falseness sustains Ivanhoe in his acceptance of the challenge. Despite his lingering injuries and the extreme weariness of his horse, the hero does not hesitate in his duty to truth: "I am a good knight and noble, come hither to sustain with lance and sword the just and lawful quarrel of this damsel, Rebecca . . . to uphold the doom pronounced against her to be false and truthless, and to defy Sir Brian de Bois-Guilbert as a traitor, murderer, and liar, as I will prove in this field with my body against his, by the aid of God, and our Lady, and of Monseigneur St. George, the good knight" (chap. 43, pp. 437–38).

Ivanhoe's faith in the truth his wounded body will reveal on the field of honor is so strong that he contemptuously refuses Bois-Guilbert's offer to delay the test. The Templar may only want the better fame of defeating a healthy Ivanhoe, but his "changed and hollow voice" suggests a less obvious motive: Bois-Guilbert senses that the falseness of his position may well be proved against him by one fighting on the side of justice. In any case, Bois-Guilbert feels the injustice of his own cause. The just cause that arms Ivanhoe makes his wounds inconsequential; he needs no time to prepare for judicial combat: "Thus—thus as I am, and not otherwise . . . it is the judgment of God—to His keeping I commend myself" (chap. 43, p. 438). Ivanhoe trusts that on the field, God will allow nothing but a fair conclusion. Rebecca need not wait upon the recovery of her champion for the recovery of her freedom.

Rebecca's redemption is especially dramatic in that it occurs after she has been found guilty by the Grand Templar's court; therefore her right to a champion serves to correct the grossly wrong verdict made against her. The danger of judicial error so evident in the examination of Waverley and in the trial of Porteous is exaggerated and at the same time made insignificant. The workings of the romance will not allow justice to be frustrated by ordinary circumstances. The marvelous aspect of Scott's resolution of the threatened injustice against Rebecca is sharpened by his realistic presentation of the trial itself. Scott narrates Rebecca's trial in a fashion becoming the author of *Letters on Demonology and Witchcraft*. That is to say, he provides a rationalistic running commentary on the tissue of lies and misinterpretations that constitute the case against Rebecca. Against the truth (Rebecca), Scott reveals the self-interest of Malvoisin (who seeks to protect Bois-Guilbert and use him to improve his position in the order of the Templars) and the cruel fanaticism of Lucas Beaumanoir (who superstitiously credits such things as demonic possession).

Scott could have modeled this threatening mixture of selfishness, ignorance, prejudice, and law upon trial scenes of his politically radical forerunners. In Jacobin fiction, political and social conditions make justice an impossible achievement for a victim of the law.[23] Although they speak against the law, the accused (in such novels as Godwin's *Caleb Williams* or Wollstonecraft's *Maria*) speak to little effect. Rebecca's address may appear no more effective, but because of her right to call for a champion, her innocence can be proved despite the forces arrayed against her. Upon Bois-Guilbert's death, Rebecca is redeemed in the eyes of all: " 'This is indeed the judgment of God,' said the Grand Master, looking upwards—'*Fiat voluntas tua!*' " (chap. 43, p. 439). Ivanhoe's valor and God's intervention, then, are quite literally an extension of Rebecca's trial rather than a repudiation of it. She is protected by powers that do not apply in the material world of the Jacobins.

Ivanhoe's victory on behalf of Rebecca is obviously like that of Sir Kenneth's over Conrad in that it reveals guilt and punishes it at the same moment. But it is also similar in that it secures innocence by discovering guilt. The same pattern prevails in our own age's romances of justice. It is sufficient in our legal system for the defense to raise a reasonable doubt of the prosecution's case; juries are to find a defendant guilty or not (proven) guilty— "innocence" need not be an issue. But doubts are not the stuff of romances of justice. Perry Mason, for example, can only acquit a client by proving another person guilty—indeed, by forcing a courtroom confession from the guilty party. Rebecca's innocence becomes apparent to all when Bois-Guilbert's guilt is dramatically revealed. Sir Kenneth fully clears himself of dishonor by publicly dishonoring Conrad. Bentham had argued that all punishment is in itself evil and, therefore, can only be justified by realizing a greater portion of social good.[24] But in *Ivanhoe* and *The Talisman* it becomes impossible to separate the intrinsic good of punishment from the extrinsic good that may be gained by its exercise. The one is too intricately bound with the other.

The final scene of punishment in *The Talisman*—Saladin's beheading of the Grand Master—encapsulates the wishes that prevail in Scott's romances of justice. It is very unlike the problematic, ambiguous, or discomforting scenes in the novels we have examined earlier. Saladin's act of just violence leaves no nagging questions as to its right or its effectiveness. Nor does it challenge the virtue of the executioner, or long disturb the conscience of those who benefit most from the deed. It punishes wrong with decisive speed and clarity. It reveals right with equal dispatch.

Exotic characters in romance are often endowed with the power to cure others. Rebecca (possessed of the mysterious and profound knowledge of the East) and Saladin (possessed of the miraculous Talisman) exercise this power. But Saladin's gift includes the ability to heal moral ills through punishment. The physician, judge, and executioner are combined in the soldan's person. The analogy of crime to illness and punishment to cure is an old and often-used one: in Plato's *Gorgias*, Socrates employs it to demonstrate that the unpunished, guilty man is more miserable than the punished.[25] After Conrad's defeat, Richard asks Saladin to play the physician in behalf of the criminal. In this case Saladin would prefer to play the judge. He thinks Conrad "is more fit to be dragged from the lists to the gallows . . . than to profit" from the Talisman's virtues (chap. 28, p. 302). Nevertheless, he consents to the wishes of his royal brother; Conrad will be restored to physical health in order to allow him adequate time for spiritual repentance. But the Grand Master, who has reason to fear Conrad's contrite mood, circumvents Richard's wish and Saladin's art: he stabs and kills his defenseless fellow conspirator.

Unknown to the Templar, his crime is witnessed by the dwarf Nectabanus, who—in a state of panic—relays what he has seen to the soldan. But Nectabanus's information is not at this time revealed to the reader; Scott turns away from the dwarf's story to note the arrival of guests at Saladin's feast. The scene quoted below, then, is intended to surprise readers as much as participants: only Saladin and Nectabanus know of the murder, and Saladin confirms the Templar's guilt by having Nectabanus repeat the words the Templar spoke as he stabbed Conrad:

> Saladin made a sign to the dwarf, who advanced and pronounced, with a harsh voice, the words "Accipe hoc!" The Templar started, like a steed who sees a lion . . . yet instantly recovered, and to hide, perhaps, his confusion, raised the goblet to his lips; but those lips never touched the goblet's rim. The sabre of Saladin left its sheath as lightning leaves the cloud. It was waved in the air, and the head of the Grand Master rolled to the extremity of the tent, while the trunk remained for a second standing, with the goblet still clenched in its grasp, then fell, the liquor mingling with the blood that spurted from the veins. (Chap. 28, p. 310)

The shock that naturally follows this execution is not of lasting force. Saladin immediately defuses fear with assurances of the general safety and a calm recital of the Grand Master's many crimes. But he identifies a defining characteristic of punishment by emphasizing that the Templar's punishment has been exacted for a specific crime—not for his general villainy. The soldan proceeds to prove that the Templar was guilty of Conrad's murder. And the evidence that he offers stands unqualified by Scott's narrative method; no editor intrudes (as in the Porteous trial) to offer conflicting evidence. Although some of the spectators remain slightly uneasy with the Templar's headless corpse beside them, the spirited and honest Richard quickly accepts the plain truth of Saladin's explanation as well as the rightness of his behavior: "we have witnessed a great act of justice, though it bore a different aspect" (chap. 28, p. 312).

By summarily beheading the Templar, Saladin personally and decisively enforces justice. His act is "great" largely in that it remains uncluttered by moral or practical qualifications. From Saladin's perspective, the Templar committed a crime and deserved to die for it. Scott's management of the execution protects rather than questions the simplicity of this justification. The Western onlookers provide no critical perspective on the "different aspect" of Saladin's justice. They do not note, for example, that the Templar's public trial occurs after his execution. Indeed there are significant unspoken advantages for them in Saladin's act; the beheading of the Grand Master does not involve those whom it should interest most. When the passive Kenneth stood before an enraged Richard, DeVaux had pleaded against the king's threats: "My liege, this must not be—here, nor by your own hand." He is relieved to take away the Scot before "Richard's descending to the unkingly act" of playing the headsman. DeVaux wants Richard to assign an executioner—to symbolize his power without sullying it. Assigning an executioner, however, only distances responsibility; it does not eliminate it. Punishment, as I noted in the introduction to this book, is never the affair of "others" who live within an established state—at least never except in fictions we choose to believe. Conveniently, none of the Western princes are home. None are asked to assent to Saladin's blow or to consider the evidence that prompts it in advance; they may only respond to its result. They need not wash their hands of the deed because they have not dirtied them.

Yet Saladin's hands also remain unsmudged. He slices through the Templar's neck as neatly as he slices a falling silken veil in a demonstration of his blade's effectiveness. Regarding that demonstration, Richard (then unaware of his physician's identity) imagines Saladin is "as expert in inflicting wounds as my sage Hakim in curing them" (chap. 27, p. 290). Saladin's surgical expertise in dispatching the Grand Master clearly suggests that he is untroubled by the odium DeVaux fears Richard would incur as Kenneth's executioner. Richard, in fact, reminds us of DeVaux's concern in his first questions to Saladin: "But wherefore in this presence? wherefore with thine own hand?" (chap. 28, p. 312). Saladin replies that he had "designed otherwise," but was hastened to act before the Templar could accept the food offered him: "if I had permitted him to taste of my cup, as he was about to do, how could I, without incurring the brand of inhospitality, have done him to death as he deserved?" By invoking the law of hospitality as reason for his sudden intervention, Saladin not only explains the act but points to yet another of its virtues. In this case the soldan serves as an ideal executioner, for he is altogether uninvolved with the criminal. The perfection of the scene, then, consists in two main points: the Western princes are distanced from the act; Saladin is distanced from the victim. Bentham's observation that the suffering of the criminal is an addition to the suffering of the community does not apply to the soldan's deft stroke, for the Grand Master shares nothing with Saladin—not even a bowl of sherbet.

Because of Saladin's separateness from all concerned, his act does not challenge the sovereignty of the Western princes. Indeed, it functions as a preventive medicine in that it saves them further internal conflict. The rulers of England, France, and Austria formed an unsteady alliance in their crusade to the Holy Land. Much of their time on that crusade is spent competing for power or, at least, defining lines of power. Crimes such as that of the Templar pose problems of jurisdiction. Who would have the right to punish the Templar? What consequences might ensue for one who would accept the responsibility? Saladin's presumption does not answer these questions so much as it dissolves them. His act of justice is open and certainly bodily, but from the perspective of the Western princes it deftly elides concerns that arise from a public display of power.

Also dissolved are the physical marks of the act itself. In *The Heart of Midlothian*, the glimpses we have of executions are unsettlingly ugly. But no one is sickened by Saladin's decisive cure. The feast he has prepared need only be briefly interrupted: "The body was carried away, and the marks of the slaughter obliterated or concealed with such dexterity, as showed that the case was not altogether so uncommon as to paralyse the assistants and officers of Saladin's household" (chap. 28, p. 312). Although the case is uncommon enough to disturb the "christian princes" in attendance, their mood seems only an inability to appreciate readily the perfection of Saladin's justice. As I noted, Richard's temperament allows him to surmount "all cause for suspicion or embarrassment."

"Embarrassment" may seem an odd word in this context; but given the "different aspect" of Saladin's justice, it is not inappropriate. Saladin's physicality exemplifies (as Alexander Welsh remarks) the special dispensation of the dark hero—the same dispensation granted Rob Roy.[26] Such characters can act with an uncensured freedom denied their properly civil counterparts. But the gift of healing by punishing operates only in the romances of justice. Rob Roy's stabbing of Rashleigh leaves Frank in undisputed possession of what turns out to be a rather melancholy, heirless estate. In contrast, Saladin's blade excises—without complications—a dangerous cancer.

The crusade, of course, is not saved; the alliance of European states cannot be held together for the goal of taking Jerusalem. But that loss should not be overestimated, for the goal is ill considered. The true responsibility of the Western leaders clearly lies in the West. Furthermore, the alliance is not dissolved in the anger, suspicion, and violence that Conrad and the Templars sought to engender. An unwise cause has simply come to a strangely quiet and proper end. Finally, it must be noted, Saladin is left to the peaceful possession of his rightful empire. To embody a still more attractive wish concerning punishment, we must conceive of a society that shuns its use altogether. There are no magical cures for wrongs in *Redgauntlet: A Tale of the Eighteenth Century*, but nor is there need for the strong medicine Saladin prescribes. Scott discovers in his romance of the recent past an even more amiable solution for the pains that afflict power at the moment pains are inflicted by power.

CHAPTER SIX

Redgauntlet as a Romance of Power

The great men in monarchies are so heavily punished by disgrace, by the loss (tho' often imaginary) of their fortune,
credit, acquaintances, and pleasures, that rigour in respect to
them is needless. It can tend only to divest the subjects of the
affection they have for the person of their prince, and of the
respect they ought to have for public posts and employments.

—Montesquieu

IN a contemporary review of *Redgauntlet* (1824), Thomas Noon
Talfourd offered a sharply negative assessment of Scott's general
achievement. The central problem of the Waverley novels as seen
from Talfourd's reformist perspective was their implied denigra-
tion of any vigorous political program. Taking up J. L. Adolphus's
complaint of the hero's passivity, Talfourd argues that Scott's
heroes owe their eventual prosperity "to their inertness and irresolution, and to a considerable dose of that political pliancy which
is well known . . . by the technical appellation of 'trimming.'"
In essence, Scott recommends by this fruitful disengagement a
"political quietism, which leaves every thing to chance, and finds
every abuse its own compensation and cure."[1]

Scott's novels of the recent past seem especially subject to Talfourd's criticism, for they are most closely aligned with the world
he so wants to change. Without an active political program, justice seems a matter of mere preservation. To put it in a slightly
different way, the conservatism of *Waverley*, *Rob Roy*, and *The
Heart of Midlothian* is especially insidious because the hero's pros-

perity is secured amidst—not against—social evil. Talfourd (an idealistic lawyer; a friend of Lamb, Hazlitt, and, later, Dickens; and an author of a tract against the use of the pillory as punishment) considers this moral irresolution to be a particularly grievous fault in *Redgauntlet*: "The inequality of the war between vice and virtue, between the designing and the unsuspecting, is too palpable; and the reader, instead of rising with new impulses of enthusiasm towards good, from the perusal, is compelled to quit the book with a hopeless depression of spirits, at the predominance of evil, and with a tame disposition to acquiesce in an order of things which appears absolutely irremediable."[2] On the side of vice Talfourd concocts an oddly assorted list of characters that includes the self-tormenting smuggler, Nanty Ewart; the treacherous Christel Nixon; the hypocritical smuggler's middleman, Thomas Trumbull; the blind fiddler, Wandering Willie; and the crazed and greedy litigant Peter Peebles. Virtue proves far more difficult to detect. The dutiful, generally passive characters cannot win Talfourd's respect; goodness for him demands "rising with new impulses of enthusiasm." The "order of things" needs reshuffling.

For those of us less engaged in the immediate political world of 1824, Talfourd's remarks on the great preponderance of evil in *Redgauntlet* must seem strange. The hero, Darsie Latimer, and his long-lost sister, Lilias, the industrious and loyal Alan Fairford, the disciplined and peaceful Joshua Geddes, his sister Rachael, and the able, polite, forgiving General Campbell appear more than a sufficient counterweight to Talfourd's examples of vice. It seems the point of difference between author and critic is that Scott assumes what Talfourd cannot accept—the virtue of the late-eighteenth-century political order of *Redgauntlet* and by extension that of his own world. From this perspective acquiescence is no depressing moral. Enthusiasm is clearly the province of those who would trouble a well-established, moderate, and prosperous system. For Scott, the Hanoverian government's goodness makes its citizens' inaction positively desirable. In addition, its goodness combined with its strength make its own inaction equally desirable: a weak, ineffective evil need not—should not—be vigorously answered by an unassailable power. The satisfying political reality that Scott projects in *Redgauntlet* makes punishment almost unnecessary; or, perhaps more accurately, the very absence of hard

punishment in *Redgauntlet* projects the vision of a satisfying political reality. In the historical context of 1824, such an expression of
confidence takes on a polemical character.

Generally in the Waverley novels we may understand the decreased use and diminished severity of punishment as a mark of
an advanced civilization. For example, in *Old Mortality* Scott as
narrator has a privileged distance from the pain that the rebel
Macbriar suffers before the Scottish privy council in 1679. The
"boot," or torture device, used on the staunch Covenanter calls
for an explanatory clause addressed to the humane and sophisticated audience of the early nineteenth century. Other examples
of primitive cruelty (the "wooden mare," the "cameronian's gibbet," the "prisoner's procession," and the "heads of the executed")
become subjects of Scott's footnotes; their distinctly antiquarian
flavor is unmistakable.[3] Henry Morton wins the blessing of history
by repudiating the cruelty of the rebels and the royalists; in the
revolution of 1688 the country catches up to his humanity. This
sense of progress is typical of Scott's historicism. Adam Ferguson
sketches a picture of civilization's potential that both Morton and
his author would approve: "So long as the majority of a people is
supposed to act on maxims of probity, the example of the good,
and even the caution of the bad, give a general appearance of in-
tegrity, and of innocence. Where men are to one another objects of
affection and of confidence, where they are generally disposed not
to offend, government may be remiss; and every person may be
treated as innocent, till he is found to be guilty."[4] In *Redgauntlet*
Scott depicts a society much like that envisioned by Ferguson: one
in which government may be "remiss" in protecting itself through
punishment, and by this kindness be all the better protected.

The tale (set in the mid-1760s) concerns the futile last effort by
a lone, fanatical Jacobite to deliver Great Britain to the Chevalier,
Charles Edward. As part of this improbable effort, Redgauntlet
kidnaps his nephew Darsie Latimer, who has been raised on the
better principles of the revolution. Redgauntlet hopes that by winning or forcing Darsie's open support, those faithful to the family
will rally to the cause. The beautifully managed, almost comic termination of this extraordinary scheme suggests that power is envisioned as most satisfying when it is represented as least active.
The state itself becomes—like the Waverly hero—a passive force.[5]

Because of this, Hugh Redgauntlet—unlike Fergus or Evan in *Waverley*, Macbriar in *Old Mortality*, or the smuggler Wilson in *The Heart of Midlothian*—cannot have his suffering display the tyranny of the opposition. On the contrary, he must accept his enemies' kindness and understand his own puny criminality.

Graham McMaster refuses to make much of *Redgauntlet*'s confident resolution. He insists that the body of the novel cannot be so briskly resolved by an unconvincing dream of an effective, rational government—an "instrument of central sanity." General Campbell "comes like a wish" and history grants no such wishes.[6] But surely the blessed quality of Campbell's appearance tells us much; we should not discount Scott's ideal because we have been taught to disbelieve it. The romance here is one of power—of evident, acknowledged, and accepted authority. This is not to say that for Scott might makes right. But in *Redgauntlet* might quite simply *is* right. Power in this novel needs no special champion like Ivanhoe, for it commands nearly universal obedience. Such credit is born of what Bertrand de Jouvenel would call a belief in power's legitimacy, a hope in its beneficence, and a consciousness of its strength;[7] together these qualities make *Redgauntlet* a novel about a rebellion that cannot happen and a punishment that does not happen. Scott's late-eighteenth-century Great Britain is a relatively comfortable place: its laws rather more like those envisioned by Blackstone than those that anger Talfourd—not perfect certainly, but (nearly all can agree) in need of wondrously little change.[8]

Such a reading of *Redgauntlet* must encounter some serious objections. As Marilyn Butler points out, Scott's happy endings generally seem precarious; the Author of *Waverley* had, after all, lived through a revolution.[9] More specifically, Scott's Great Britain of 1824 encouraged little of the confidence that I find in the novel. The memory of the Peterloo massacre (1819) and the factors that led to that event could not be wholly erased by the ensuing few years of widespread economic revival. And men like Talfourd were still possessed with reforming zeal. Even if the political climate had cooled somewhat, literary people remained a contentious group. William Hazlitt (in the same year as Talfourd and in the same *New Monthly Magazine*) passionately lamented Scott's blindness to the present despite his insight into the past.[10] And six years after Scott's death (and six years after the first reform bill) Carlyle wrote Scott off as a man without a message in an age that desperately needed a message.[11] For his own part, Scott was not calmly assured concerning his society's direction or stability. His letters and journal betray persistent fears for the survival of the world he knew and loved.[12] Finally, *Redgauntlet* itself (as McMaster so well points out) is not without its dark undercurrent. The law seems a petty, clumsy matter in respect to the Peter Peebles episode—perhaps even, as David Brown puts it, a mere "parasite of the property system."[13] The richest smuggler is the one most secure from prosecution. And the interests of efficiency and tradition clash on the banks of the Solway as the spearfishers destroy the tide nets of Joshua Geddes.

But a romance may overcome even such obstacles as these; it is a form that privileges broad, conservative sympathies over upsetting details. In short, Scott's wishes preempt his fears. Scott's unwillingness to accept disturbing fears (or facts) in the fiction of *Redgauntlet* is indicated by the defensive quality in a crucial passage of his 1832 Introduction to that novel.[14] He first recalls the rebellion of 1745 as a "civil war . . . remembered by the existing generation without any degree of the bitterness of spirit which seldom fails to attend internal dissension" (p. ix). Such generosity is encouraged by the sharp decline of Jacobite enthusiasm. In essence, only one side remains, except for those old men of "warm imaginations and weak understandings" who sustained the faith long beyond the defeat at Culloden. These misguided few were combated by the policy of Sir Robert Walpole, who adopted a "very prudential and humane line of conduct" in order to allow a foolish cause to die of its own inherent weakness (p. xi).

In one instance, however, the government departed from its enlightened policy of leniency. Scott's apology for that departure is instructive in light of what occurs in the novel itself. Dr. Archibald Cameron (the brother of a notorious Jacobite, and an exile for his part in the rebellion) was arrested in Scotland in 1751. Scott summarizes the public's understanding of his case as follows:

> Dr. Cameron had never borne arms, although engaged in the Rebellion, but used his medical skill for the service, indifferently, of the wounded of both parties. His return to Scotland was ascribed exclusively to family affairs. His behavior at the bar was decent, firm, and

respectful. His wife threw herself on three different occasions, before George II. and the members of his family, was rudely repulsed
from their presence, and at length placed, it was said, in the same
prison with her husband, and confined with unmanly severity.

Dr. Cameron was finally executed, with all the severities of the
law of treason; and his death remains in popular estimation a dark
blot upon the memory of George II., being almost publicly imputed
to a mean and personal hatred of Donald Cameron of Lochiel, the
sufferer's heroic brother. (Pp. xi–xii)

But in a provocative and telling move away from the details of
the commonly accepted version, Scott goes on to fault the king's
ministers for the public's misperception of the facts: George II is
removed from all censure.

In taking this line of defense, Scott adopts a position similar to
one often championed a century and a half earlier on behalf of the
Stuarts: if wrong exists, look to blame anyone but the king. Of
course we have often revived and adjusted such reasoning in our
own time and country, for our own purposes. Whether in 1677,
1824, or today, these variations serve to protect a central authority
against challenges from those who would shift or disperse the center. Cameron, Scott reveals, did not return to the Highlands on
mere private business; his execution could "certainly have been
justified, had the King's ministers so pleased, upon reasons of a
public nature" (p. xii). The ministry chose to keep quiet regarding
Cameron's dangerous purpose in order to preserve the value of
their knowledge of the rebels' lines of communication. The king's
character, then, unjustly suffers as a result of an understandable,
but "ill advised and ungenerous . . . policy of the administration"
(p. xii). Scott favors leniency as a solution to the conflicting demands of justice, secrecy, and what might be called public relations. Much good could have been "gained by sparing the life of
Dr. Cameron after conviction, and limiting his punishment to per-
petual exile" (p. xii).

Because Scott centers his discussion of the Cameron case on
the government's control of the people's response to it—on the
appearance of guilt rather than the substance—justice here becomes a side issue. He is concerned about not what punishment
the rebel most deserves, but what punishment best serves the
government's complicated interests. This instrumentalist view of

punishment is typical of the eighteenth century. As J. M. Beattie points out, the theory of deterrence that prevailed in the sentences passed down by judges of that time did not require consistency— or what we would call justice.[15] Decisions of death did, however, require some sensitivity to the public's idea of necessity; Scott seems to understand that the actual execution of Cameron "with all the severities of the law of treason" (that is to say, hanging and dismemberment) undermines the very power it expresses; it expends or wastes power rather than extends or saves it.

Foucault helps us appreciate the significance of this adjustment in the exercise of power by concentrating on the expressive or symbolic function of punishment. He insists that executions whether presented in reality or in print exhibit "the intersection of the excess of armed justice and the anger of the threatened people." Leniency becomes, therefore, a new "technique of power"—a way of avoiding dangerous ceremonies of suffering.[16] In this instance, Scott's language anticipates Foucault's historical conjecture as to the meaning of the transition from the body to the soul as the locus of punishment; reasons of a purely "public nature" provide the sole grounds both to justify and to criticize the ministry's decision. No position regarding the act of execution need consider the rebel's character or moral responsibility. No position need consider the government's right or the justice of its action. But any position must take into account the message it shapes. The message of the Cameron execution is clearly an undesirable one from the standpoint of those who design it and hope to benefit by it.

The literature of the gallows (as Foucault explains) embodies the shifting awareness on the part of power concerning its own interests. Two sides of public execution are naively expressed by these texts. On one hand, their confessional, moralistic tenor serves as a kind of propaganda. They provide an affirmation of the court's judgment or a lesson on better (and safer) ways to live. On the other hand, the texts dramatize the scope of the criminal's "tiny struggle" against power and project that struggle as a heroic and even epic undertaking.[17] Scott's novels, of course, greatly surpass such broadsheets in both scope and sophistication; nevertheless, they do reveal similarly equivocal tensions in respect to crime and punishment.[18]

Conflicting messages (as in the execution of Fergus and Evan

Dhu in *Waverley*) or a perhaps consciously uncertain perspective (as in the lynching/hanging of Porteous in *The Heart of Midlothian*) functions to complicate execution scenes in many of the Scottish Waverley novels. As I have shown in Chapter 5, such tensions are alleviated in *Ivanhoe* and *The Talisman*, where the message of sanctioned killing is sharply clarified and controlled by recourse to a simple faith in the inevitability of justice. But in *Redgauntlet* Scott takes still another approach. In this, his last major novel of Scotland's postrevolutionary history, he resolves the tension of the government's response to illegality by portraying power's kindness. The Cameron episode is contained within the introduction. No such incident occurs in the novel proper. The gentle resolution Scott constructs allows Charles Edward to return to France and freely permits the rebels either to follow their prince into exile or to redefine their loyalties. Nearly all accept the second choice. This serene close identifies power's best interests with its most modest expressions.

Obedience to this benign force makes citizens as discreet as the government they serve. Alan Fairford, for example, defines "civil courage" as a necessary virtue of the day. Such courage primarily concerns fair dealings in financial matters: that is, the courage not to cheat for profit. In regard to a more purely physical brand of courage, "it is of little consequence to most men in this age and country whether they even possess military courage or no" (letter 5, p. 40). The Quaker Joshua Geddes makes a point of repressing the military part of his courage: he finds that "enduring" requires as much strength as "acting." And it must also be noted that Geddes finds enduring quite profitable. But lest we suspect Geddes's honest passivity on account of his good fortune, Darsie Latimer (who narrates portions of the novel) offers a telling judgment on the Quaker's bearing in comparison to that of the strange and stern Redgauntlet: "as they sat fronting each other, I could not help thinking that they might have formed no bad emblem of Peace and War" (letter 6, p. 50).

Geddes, it must be noted, receives inadequate protection for his tide nets; but for a novel mainly concerned with a rebellious undertaking, the Great Britain of *Redgauntlet* seems very secure—indeed peaceful. Despite suggestions of scattered public discontent and the vigorous strength and fanatical loyalty of Redgauntlet, the Jacobite cause never seems more than an eccentric gambit—inconsequential to the established order. Rumors of "threatening intrigues" are never given substance by the novel's action. Darsie cannot but think "that the government would scarce, at this time of day, be likely to proceed against any one even of the most obnoxious rebels" (letter 7, p. 70). He remembers "old ladies of family over their hyson, and grey-haired lairds over their punch . . . utter a little harmless treason." And he adds the obvious point, "the disaffection of such persons was too unimportant to excite the attention of government" (chap. 8, p. 216).

Redgauntlet attempts to cut through this comfortable habit of mind by appealing to Darsie to take "noble revenge" against those who killed his father for his part in the rebellion of 1745: "His skull is yet standing over the Rikargate, and even its bleak and mouldered jaws command you to be a man. I ask you, in the name of God and of your country, will you draw your sword and go with me to Carlisle, were it but to lay your father's head, now the perch of the obscene owl and carrion crow, and the scoff of every ribald clown, in consecrated earth, as befits his long ancestry?" (chap. 19, p. 363). But even such familial passion fails to influence Darsie, who remains firmly on the side of prudence and passivity. He disregards the "command" of his father's rotting skull as easily as Waverley forgets the severed head of Fergus atop the same gate at Carlisle. Even if Darsie were persuaded by the justice of the cause (which he is not), he would insist on "some reasonable hope of success." An execution distanced by twenty-some years of a father he cannot remember does nothing to change Darsie's vision of the immediate state of affairs:

> "I look around me, and I see a settled government—an established authority—a born Briton on the throne—the very Highland mountaineers, upon whom alone the trust of the exiled family reposed, assembled into regiments, which act under the orders of the existing dynasty. France has been utterly dismayed by the tremendous lessons of the last war, and will hardly provoke another. All without and within the kingdom is adverse to encountering a hopeless struggle, and you alone, sir, seem willing to undertake a desperate enterprise." (Chap. 19, p. 364)

Perhaps the difference between this vision and the one offered to Waverley just after the battle of Culloden makes Darsie less annoyingly passive than his prototype. In any case, the basis for his loyalty is well fixed. His biological father a mere abstraction, Darsie is able to adopt without reservation a safer line of descent. He acts (or does not act) with a consistent appreciation of the obligations he has incurred by living under Hanoverian rule.[19]

Redgauntlet's "strange delusion" regarding the forces of discontent he may command for his purpose is further reduced by Scott in several scenes before it is finally undone by the government's mercy. For example, the crazed Peter Peebles remembers the start of his hopelessly tangled lawsuit by reference to the rebellion of 1745. In making this connection he suggests a likeness between his consuming madness and that of the most stubborn rebels.[20] In another scene, Darsie's sister Lilias tells of the absurdly outdated challenge offered George III upon his coronation. The king disregards the chivalric gesture from both "prudence" and "lenity," although Redgauntlet persists in interpreting his "forbearance" as a sign of cowardice (chap. 18, p. 352). Nanty Ewart provides the most explicit belittling of the rebels' dreams with his shrewd judgment on their prospects as he upbraids Fairford for what he wrongly supposes is the young lawyer's Jacobite mission: "All these rackets and riots that you think are trending your way have no relation at all to your interest; and the best way to make the whole kingdom friends again at once would be the alarm of such an undertaking as these mad old fellows are trying to launch into" (chap. 14, p. 298).

Nanty's remark on the effects of the Jacobite scare applies well to the effects Scott manages at the close of *Redgauntlet*; the narrative of alarm and response do much to make friends of factions. The mood is in some respects akin to that expressed by the close of Scott's third novel, *The Antiquary*. In that tale, set in the late eighteenth century, the whole country rallies against the threat (which turns out to be nonexistent) of a French invasion. In *Redgauntlet*, however, there is not even an imagined enemy from without, and from within the most committed Jacobites must ultimately be resigned to an honorable surrender of their hopes. The work's last two chapters convey this sense of unanimity and well deserve the high praise they generally receive. Each develops a significant anticlimax that displays and secures the government's power.

The first occurs as the rebellious Jacobites are forced to understand the essential falseness of their ambitions. As a condition for their support of the Stuart cause they insist that Charles Edward remove his mistress—a suspected agent of Walpole—from his royal society. Charles not only refuses but ignores their request: "Conditions can have no part betwixt prince and subject" (chap. 22, p. 407). Only Redgauntlet can accept such a flat assertion of absolutism. The revealed disagreement between prince and subject provides a much-desired exit for those cool, slightly embarrassed characters who find that their nostalgia cannot sustain their zeal at the moment of crisis. For those like Sir Richard Glendale, who act upon nobler sentiments, Charles's refusal brings into question long-held royalist principles. As A. O. J. Cockshut points out, Glendale discovers to his surprise that he is in fact a good constitutional monarchist.[21] By the end of the penultimate chapter, the extent of the planned uprising has shrunk from a nationwide rebellion to a simple desire to return Charles Edward safely to France.

The final chapter, however, briefly rekindles Redgauntlet's ambitious hopes before totally destroying them in a display of Hanoverian grace and power. When the Jacobites learn that the ship intended for Charles Edward's escape has sailed, they consider themselves bound by honor to accept Redgauntlet's zealous call: "let despair renew the union amongst us which accident disturbed" (chap. 23, p. 424). But before he can speak another sentence, a greater reason for despair dampens his flickering hopes. News of an unsuspected treachery makes it clear that the cause cannot even begin with the slightest hope of success:

> "I give my voice for displaying the royal banner instantly, and—How now!" he concluded, sternly, as Lilias . . . put into his hand the scroll, and added, it was designed for that of Nixon.
> Redgauntlet read, and, dropping it on the ground, continued to stare upon the spot where it fell with raised hands and fixed eyes. Sir Richard Glendale lifted the fatal paper, read it, and saying, "Now all is indeed over," handed it to Maxwell, who said aloud, "Black Colin Campbell, by G——d!" (Chap. 23, p. 424)

But the cause is to be defeated in a way no Jacobite—least of all Redgauntlet—suspects. Even a hopeless cause can retain a living identity. As I have noted, a violent expression of the state's force may easily call attention to itself as a threat to individual citizens. But in *Redgauntlet* power expresses itself more subtly and effectively.

The much-feared Colin Campbell does arrive backed by a considerable force, but he walks alone among the desperate plotters: "Amid this scene of confusion, a gentleman, plainly dressed in a riding-habit, with a black cockade in his hat, but without any arms except a *couteau-de-chasse*, walked into the apartment without ceremony. He was a tall, thin, gentlemanly man, with a look and bearing decidedly military. He had passed through their guards, if in the confusion they now maintained any, without stop or question, and now stood almost unarmed among armed men, who, nevertheless, gazed on him as on the angel of destruction" (chap. 23, p. 425). Campbell turns out to be a good angel. His almost magical presence here dispels one dream and replaces it with another; it repudiates a world of heroic gestures and ushers in a world of calm and settled unanimity. George Levine sees this "transformation of heroic action into dream" as the primary subject of *Redgauntlet*.[22] Dispensing or accepting pain would be too heroic for the effect of calm disengagement that Scott desires as the end of his fiction. To some degree, Levine provides a modern variation on the complaint Talfourd made against Scott's political values, or what Talfourd took to be his lack of political values. Certainly Redgauntlet expects yet does not receive something concretely objectionable from his enemies; he supposes Campbell has the Jacobites "penned up like sheep for the slaughter," but nothing so unpleasantly crude is planned.

Campbell acts as an emissary of the king's "kind purposes." He seeks information concerning no one, intends harm to no one. He merely asks that the Jacobites grant by their passive resignation the unshakable reality of the established order. Campbell speaks the "King's very words, from his very lips" (and we might note that although Campbell has some of his own words to add, the transition from the king's voice to the voice of his representative seems hardly important):

"'I will,' said his Majesty, 'deserve the confidence of my subjects by reposing my security in the fidelity of the millions who acknowledge my title—in the good sense and prudence of the few who continue, from the errors of education, to disown it.' His Majesty will not even believe that the most zealous Jacobites who yet remain can nourish a thought of exciting a civil war, which must be fatal to their families and themselves, besides spreading bloodshed and ruin through a peaceful land. He cannot even believe of his kinsman that he would engage brave and generous, though mistaken, men in an attempt which must ruin all who have escaped former calamities; and he is convinced that, did curiousity or any other motive lead that person to visit this country, he would soon see it was his wisest course to return to the continent; and his Majesty compassionates his situation too much to offer any obstacle to his doing so." (Chap. 23, p. 427)

Redgauntlet can hardly believe his plots are subject to such easy forgiveness or unconcern as the government expresses. But when the reality of the act strikes him, he knows its meaning: " 'Then, gentlemen,' said Redgauntlet, clasping his hands together as the words burst from him, 'the cause is lost for ever!' " (chap. 23, p. 427).

It only remains for Charles Edward's stubborn but defeated adherents to escort him to the ship provided for his departure. General Campbell—still alone—goes with them to ensure the safety of the Pretender. Only Redgauntlet chooses to depart with him. All the others return to their homes and thereby change their allegiance to the reigning monarch. On the evidence of the final chapter, it appears that the allegiance is well deserved. Even Nanty Ewart's killing of Redgauntlet's disloyal servant Nixon functions to preserve the government's virtue: " 'That sound broadsword cut' said the General, 'has saved us the shame of rewarding a traitor' " (chap. 23, p. 429). Apparently a traitor to one side can be no more than a contemptible slave to the other. More importantly, however, Campbell's words on Nixon's death emphasize the point of the government's policy: the king's mercy makes the rebels themselves something other than traitors. Mistakes in judgment or education are possible, but true opposition on the part of honorable men against the established power is officially unthinkable. Civilization maintains its poise by grounding itself in the "fidelity" of the vast majority, and the "prudence" of those few who cannot conjure within themselves such a feeling.

But the novel's final pages also make it clear that Redgauntlet and Charles Edward accept the government's gentle expression of power as a kind of punishment. Both suffer the contempt of neglect

at the hands of an old enemy. Yet neither is allowed to feel the satisfaction of anger when met by the effectiveness of this unexpect-
edly gentle policy. Redgauntlet confesses himself "justly punished
by this final termination" of his views, and for "having been too
little scrupulous in the means" of realizing them. The Chevalier
especially appreciates Campbell's tact and courtesy: "You have
taught me the principle on which men on the scaffold feel forgiveness and kindness for their executioner" (chap. 23, p. 421).
Charles Edward here ironically invokes an image of the scaffold
that effectively underscores the coercive force of politic kindness.
The motives and power of the government are exposed even as
the gentleness of its means is acknowledged. Despite his gracious
words, Charles still holds to the position of the wronged party,
but his "forgiveness and kindness" toward his punisher make clear
that he will never again entertain thoughts of reversing his fate.
The punishment, then, works to secure a peaceful submission to
the government's power. As Campbell says, "It is now all over . . .
and Jacobite will no longer be a party name" (chap. 23, p. 430).

Robert Gordon finds the closing chapter of *Redgauntlet* to be
Scott's most fully realized "quest for reconciliation and peace." The
longing that Gordon discerns in *The Bride of Lammermoor* for a
"presence and assumed authority beyond the reach even of the
rhetoric of Burke" is nearly captured in this late novel of Hanoverian solidity.[23] For the most part, I agree with Gordon's assessment, but it may be useful to consider more carefully the substance
of Scott's imaginative transcendence and its relevance to the government's exercise of power in its suspended threat of punishment.
The king's speech relayed through the voice of Campbell claims the
force of popular will as the basis of a new and more effective, secularized royalism. The security of the royal sovereignty reposes in
the people. Such security permits and even encourages liberality
toward wrongdoers. In this respect, Scott's vision of the potential
benevolence of a powerfully grounded, popular authority is similar to one expressed by Beccaria, the Enlightenment reformer of
criminal law and punishment: "while the laws reign tranquilly, in
a form of government enjoying the consent of the entire nation,
well defended externally and internally by force, and by opinion,
which is perhaps even more efficacious than force, where executive
power is lodged with the true sovereign alone . . . I see no neces-

sity for destroying a citizen."[24] Buried in Beccaria's description of
the conditions that allow civil kindness is a clause that hints at
another version of the same scaffold that Charles Edward alludes
to. A large amount of coercion is involved in penal lenity; a strong
internal and external defense precedes or is at least concomitant
with the rejection of capital punishment.

Bertrand de Jouvenel's analysis of the growth of power suggests
further advantages inherent in the fiction of a popularly founded
sovereignty. Once it is assumed that the people themselves invest
rulers with the right to rule, the people in effect surrender all
rights. As I have noted, Scott's heroes often discover the threatening consequences of their surrender. Yet paradoxically the divine
authority claimed by the Stuarts proves far less potent than the
popular authority claimed by George III. Jouvenel invokes Hobbes
in explaining the growth of this "despotism from the principles of
Popular Sovereignty": because the sovereign merely represents
each individual, no individual can be wronged by the sovereign.[25]
Of course Jouvenel hardly intended George III as an example of
the advantage power has taken of popular assent. Neither could
Scott have (in 1824) believed in an effective and complete change
to a new structure of authority. As Francis Hart points out, Scott
must have felt the decline of the monarchy and with that decline
the crisis of authority in transition.[26] Surely, it is the fate of our
own century to appreciate fully the crises resulting from completed
transitions. But Scott's actual uncertainties make his dreams no
less instructive. The transcendence Gordon finds in *Redgauntlet*
is powerfully felt if only briefly sustained.[27]

As is clear from his reference to Hobbes, Jouvenel's argument
suggests a fiction meaningful specifically to punishment's role in
the growth of power. If the individual identifies his will as part of
the sovereign will, the government's responsibility to punish can
be understood as a directive of the individual. In effect, the criminal can be supposed the author of his own punishment. Foucault's
explanation of the logic underlying modern forms of symbolic punishments bears some relationship to this fiction of the individual's
demanding his own punishment and may be seen at work in the
final chapter of *Redgauntlet*: "the law must appear to be a necessity of things, and power must act while concealing itself beneath
the gentle force of nature."[28] In *Redgauntlet*, the monarch's power

is not exactly concealed, nor does Campbell invoke the law since he acts precisely to avoid its unpleasantness; but the sense of inevitability, of kindly coercion, is evident in the government's policy toward the would-be rebels.

Kindness is possible and desirable largely because the government projected by this romance is so secure that it need not be aggressive in its own defense. The rebels' machinations hurt no one. The only offense offered is to those who refuse to take offense. Therefore, George III may freely pardon. But the royal prerogative is sharply limited when real harm is done to subjects. In order to examine these harder cases, we must briefly return to the first of Scott's fictions of rebellion and suppression and further consider the problem created by the individual's surrender to a collective sovereignty—a surrender that both endangers and delivers Edward Waverley. Darsie Latimer is not exposed to and saved by established power in the uneasy way of his fictional predecessor. The public good that seemed so intangible in *Waverley* finds confident expression in the gentlemanly address of General Campbell. But even in *Waverley* a suggestion appears of Scott's wishful belief in the government's essential goodness. For when forgiveness is not possible, when unkind laws must be exercised, the "necessity of things" is invoked to deliver government from the odium of responsibility.

In the climactic trial scene of *Waverley*, the judge feels great compassion for Fergus's loyal servant Evan Dhu. Leniency depends upon nothing more than the prudent repentance of the accused. Mercy awaits only Evan's recognition and acceptance of the obvious: the insurrection has failed and will never be effectively revived. Evan's unregenerate violence forces the judge to pronounce the doom. In effect, he consciously demands his own execution when he asks not for grace but for the opportunity to carry on the battle: the judge responds that Evan's "blood be upon his own head" (chap. 68, p. 321). Evan seems to realize that the government's severity exists as the only symbol available to him of his own seriousness. Significantly, Redgauntlet is allowed no such symbol. Against the scene of Evan's violent and proud defiance we should place Redgauntlet's promise to sink his sword "forty fathoms deep in the wide ocean." Although he is not less loyal or courageous than Evan, the old Jacobite's rebellious energies can find no means of expression in defeat. The government will not give him a gallows for a stage.

In a final variation of the romance of power Scott takes the potentially dangerous, uncontrolled, theatrical element out of an execution made necessary by the criminal. His short story "The Two Drovers," published in 1827 as part of the *Chronicles of the Canongate*, builds upon an opposition between the romance of power's essential kindness and an equally potent feeling of its overmastering, difficult responsibilities. The story tells in a simple, direct, and powerful fashion of a murder of an Englishman by a Scot and the Scot's consequent trial and punishment under English law. The crime arises from a clash between Highland and English prejudice. Robin Oig kills in cold anger stirred by Henry Wakefield's ignorant contempt of Scottish pride. The judge summarizes the case and passes a reluctant judgment on the Scot's responsibility. In doing so, he splits the emotional center of the story; by his passionate sincerity the judge commands as much sympathy as the man he condemns. More importantly, he (unlike the criminal) commands our approval.

The judge appreciates the complexity of motives operating in the murder; he sympathetically grants Robin Oig a kind of misguided nobility; he understands the shame the Highlander sought to purge by a stab of his dirk. But cultural forces cannot cancel out the fact of Robin's premeditated killing of his English friend. However unwittingly rude they may be, citizens such as Wakefield must be protected from the wild, individual justice that Robin exacts. Despite his own deep pity for Robin, the judge—with tears in his eyes—asserts the utilitarian necessity of the death sentence: "Englishmen have their angry passions as well as Scots; and should this man's action remain unpunished, you may unsheath . . . a thousand daggers betwixt the Land's End and the Orkneys" (chap. 2, p. 347).

Neither does Robin expect his culturally conditioned sense of honor to deliver him from the hangman. In fact, that very sense of honor requires him to pay back Wakefield's death with his own life. Kant uses the aftermath of the Scottish rebellion of 1745 to illustrate what he considers the leveling virtue of capital punishment. Persons of great courage who were motivated by honor to fight for Charles Edward would be punished too much by little pains. Penal servitude and the disgrace that accompanies it ill suits such noble characters. Contemptible characters, however, who acted out of self-interest would not be adequately punished with any pain but death. For such people, existence takes absolute precedence over honor.[29]

In these terms Robin not only deserves to be executed for his crime but deserves to be executed in recognition of his ill-founded nobility. Any lesser punishment would demean Robin, for it would imply that he acted without a full sense of his responsibility; it would lend credence to those who accuse him of cowardice. Robin's sense of retribution balances and completes the judge's wisdom: "He met his fate with great firmness, and acknowledged the justice of his sentence. But he repelled indignantly the observations of those who accused him of attacking an unarmed man. 'I give a life for the life I took,' he said, 'and what can I do more?'" (chap. 2, p. 347). In this final reflection on the justice of his punishment, Robin makes himself, not Wakefield, the unarmed man; for Robin purposefully steps outside the protection of the law. His death, then, finishes his struggle for honor and justice. It seems almost an incidental matter that his death also serves a utilitarian purpose of the state.

Together, judge and criminal offer a dramatically effective and emotionally uncluttered justification of the death penalty. Necessity and justice seem in perfect agreement. But Scott knows better than to test this resolution; he has learned from the lesson of *Waverley*. Robin's words of acceptance—not his actual physical acceptance—end the story. Scott's narrative does not make the reader a spectator to an execution. If power cannot indulge its own kind impulses as it does in *Redgauntlet*, then it must make its cruel expressions private. It was not until 1868 that the curtain was drawn upon public executions—upon stark, open displays of power. In his late imaginative visions of the recent past, Scott seems to anticipate this time and, curiously enough, our own.

Postscript on the Prison

IF Scott's novels in some way anticipate the privacy of the modern execution, it may be that they suggest as well a more significant administrative development in criminal punishment that I have left largely unconsidered: the prison. Following Foucault, much attention has been paid to the novel as an imaginative projection of ideas that later take shape in concrete civil reality; that is to say, prisons get built only after writers have shaped a cultural environment that demands them. John Bender's richly provocative *Imagining the Penitentiary: Fiction and the Architecture of Mind in Eighteenth-Century England* carries out this thesis with great energy and learning. David Miller's densely argued *The Novel and the Police* provides a slightly less ambitious but related study of nineteenth-century preoccupations with supervision.[1] Poised in history between the novelists Bender addresses and those who concern Miller stands Scott. His absence from both books prompts me to qualify in a rather specific way the new historicists' reading of the prison as the logical extension of the controlling characteristics of modern society.

Narrative for Scott implies movement. The prison, quite obviously, limits what he would consider the novelistic resources of variety in character and incident. Indeed, Scott seems keenly aware of the prison's threat to his art as a storyteller. Only death more emphatically denies the possibilities of narrative action. The prison as setting excludes Scott from his subject and leaves his narrative with nowhere to go. Robert Gordon maintains that the principal characteristic of Scott's prose style is that it complements a progressive narrative movement. It conveys the sense "that every human action is a tentative reaching-out towards an obscure future."[2] In *Peveril of the Peak*, Scott makes it clear that a prison is no place for such movement: "the thoughts and occurrences of a prison are too uniform for a narrative, and we must now convey our readers into a more bustling scene" (chap. 36, p. 430). Recent academic scholarship has been content to dwell upon, if not in, the prison, but Scott does not return to Julian Peveril's cell until the hero is ready to leave it.

In *Peveril* the reader may be thankful to escape the cell (even if Julian cannot come along), since for nearly three chapters Scott depends upon Julian's loquacious cell mate and a mysterious nocturnal visitor to keep things entertaining. Neither device succeeds very well. But Scott's narrative values do not operate apart from larger concerns. Scott's conspicuous avoidance of prison meditation (he does not avoid all forms of meditation) must be seen in a political context. Notably absent in these prison chapters are any extended reflections by the hero on his predicament. Julian fails to draw significant political meaning from his experience. Apparently, solitary prison reflections provide an untempting mode to a novelist of conservative sympathies. Julian's unfocused musings on his situation of "anxiety and danger" sustain only two short paragraphs before the diminutive figure of Sir Geoffrey Hudson compels the hero's attention "almost in spite of himself" (chap. 34, p. 399). Geoffrey's power to "compel" the hero's attention serves to accentuate the limits of Julian's reflective or critical powers, for Geoffrey is rather tedious company.

One suspects that Nigel Olifant, the hero of *The Fortunes of Nigel*, would be better able to reflect meaningfully on his situation than Julian. But Scott allows him little chance to bear out the suspicion. For one paragraph Nigel amuses himself "with the melancholy task of deciphering the names, mottoes, verses, and hieroglyphics with which his predecessors in captivity had covered the walls of their prison-house" (chap. 28, p. 337). But Nigel adds nothing to this "record of lamentation and mourning"; he does not even have the opportunity: "Lord Glenvarloch [Nigel] was interrupted by the sudden opening of the door of this prison-room. It was the warder, who came to inform him that, by order of the lieutenant of the Tower, his lordship was to have the society and attendance of a fellow-prisoner in his place of confinement" (chap.

28, p. 337). In addition to this fellow prisoner (who turns out to be Margaret Ramsey, Nigel's future bride, disguised as a boy) a host of visitors descends upon Nigel: Master Christie, George Heriot, Sir Mungo Malagrowther, and Richie Monopolies all intrude upon Nigel's solitude. Yet they would be welcome if it were not for the accusations they bring against him, for Nigel finds solitude "nearly as irksome as the company of Sir Mungo" (chap. 30, p. 371). Scott's comically desperate readiness to deliver Nigel from solitude indicates that he shares his hero's sense of its irksomeness. By avoiding Nigel's thoughts, Scott avoids what would surely be a subject of those thoughts: injustice.

Scott was, after all, responding to contemporary literary modes that were more self-consciously subversive than those generally considered by Bender or Miller. Incarceration may be turned (at least in novels) to active repudiation by the state's victim. As I have noted in regard to scenes of execution, an expression of civil power often becomes an ironic means to project a sense of the individual's sanctity against the repressive forces of social control. In Godwin's *Caleb Williams* or Mary Wollstonecraft's *Maria*, private suffering takes on explicit public significance. Nigel has no chance to decipher the messages written on the walls that surround him, but the prisoners of Jacobin novels plainly discern the lesson of their imprisonment and announce that lesson to the reader. Caleb consults his heart and comes to a radical conclusion about the prison: "This is society. This is the object, the distribution of justice, which is the end of human reason. For this sages have toiled, and the midnight oil has been wasted. This!"[3]

Wollstonecraft makes the same point even more insistently. Her substantial prison of rock and iron takes on a metaphoric dimension from the very start. Maria has always been imprisoned by the "partial laws and customs" of society and grows to consider the world a "vast prison."[4] Maria's guard Jemima enforces the connection between the world outside and the world inside the prison. Jemima was born in a "wretched garret." When she was nine days old she was consigned with other children to "two cellar-like apartments."[5] As an adult, she finds that the brothel, the hospital, the house of correction, and the workhouse defeat what little independence she claims. As Maria observes, through poverty and injustice the mind itself is "imprisoned in its own little tenement."[6]

Still another tradition may be mentioned that further compli-
cates the metaphorical dimensions of the prison and further removes it from submerged or unconsciously expressed themes of
supervision or control. As Victor Brombert points out, the cell and
the sanctuary converge in the romantic prison. Personal identity
and liberty are often discovered in restraint; given the repressive
nature of social institutions, withdrawal may be seen as the only
gesture of freedom available to the individual. Such a gesture is
greatly extended by Stendhal, whose hero Fabrice from *La Char-
treuse de Parme* makes a distinction between social or political
reality and personal identity that enables him to find freedom in
renunciation. Stendhal works from what for Scott would be an unthinkable paradox; as Brombert notes, Stendhal's prison serves
simultaneously as a symbol of pervasive tyranny and as an entry
to private joy.[7]

But this romantic myth of personal growth separate from social
context seems as alien to Scott as the Jacobin spirit of political attack. Apolitical poetic meditation for Scott is also unsatisfying. His
prisoners—his Julians and Nigels—cannot find freedom within
themselves. Unlike Shelley's Prometheus, they cannot break their
bonds by asserting an innate supremacy over them. Scott's characters must define themselves in relation to their society. And the
prisoner is denied all necessary points of reference: name, family,
property, reputation. Julian Peveril's request to share a cell with
his father meets a telling refusal: "In this place we know nothing
of fathers and sons" (chap. 36, p. 430). Surely a place that knows
nothing of descent—of social continuity and social identity—offers
little for a novelist like Scott.

Of course, the prison need not be so literal a place as I have
defined it here. Bender's argument, for example, ranges widely
over eighteenth-century fiction to consider how narratives—like
prisons—order experience in a purposefully moral fashion; he also
relates narrative to the creation of personal identity.[8] Miller sees
the novelist (and the reader) as positioned in a central, controlling place of observation in a Panopticonic world.[9] But a narrower
analysis yields benefits: remembering the prison as a place of concrete and steel (as opposed to imagining it as an abstract idea
through narrative) leads to fresh reflections upon our own uneasy
regard for the institution and its relationship to fiction. We should

remember that things happen in novels. The common sense of our culture has long been that things like reformation or moral education do not happen in prisons. The prison, then, as an imaginative construction is most akin to the endings of narratives—or at least to the endings of conventional British novels of the nineteenth century.[10]

In this regard, the idea of the prison has great force in application to Scott. At the close of *The Bride of Lammermoor*, the heroine, Lucy Ashton, retreats in madness to the corner of her bridal chamber, from which she is moved to a "more retired apartment . . . , secured as her situation required, and closely watched" (chap. 34, p. 303); the hero, Ravenswood (Lucy's lover, who has been rejected by the Ashton family in favor of a wealthier rival), dies entrapped by the liquid sands of Kelpie's Flow (chap. 35, p. 312). But significantly, the ends of the more typical, "happier" Waverley novels generally convey something unsatisfying in the domestic arrangements they achieve, for these works also project a lifeless sameness or fixity reminiscent of the prison.[11] When it becomes clear that the characters have found their proper places—their proper mates—the narratives lose force, the characters lose our interest. Most affectingly, we as readers lose the sense of a dynamic historical moment and are left with a sense of social disengagement. Instead of actively feeling time, readers are left doing time. It is a mark of Scott's achievement as a novelist of historical process that we so sharply register the difference.

Notes

Introduction

1. *A Collection of Scarce and Valuable Tracts, on the Most Interesting and Entertaining Subjects: But chiefly such as relate to the History and Constitution of these Kingdoms*, 2d ed., ed. Walter Scott (London: T. Cadell and W. Davies, 1815), 13:91.

2. Except for citations of *Waverley*, I refer throughout to the 25-volume Dryburgh Edition of *The Waverley Novels* (London and Edinburgh: Adam and Charles Black, 1893–94). For convenient reference to other editions, I cite chapter as well as page numbers.

3. As I noted in the Preface, the last officially sanctioned, extended display of the body of an executed man to take place in Great Britain occurred in 1832. See Leon Radzinowicz, *A History of English Criminal Law and Its Administration from 1750* (London: Stevens and Sons, 1948), 1:219–20.

4. Given the popularity Scott enjoyed in the nineteenth century and the respect he commanded as a literary figure, it seems surprising that a "renewal" of interest is necessary—especially when one considers that Alexander Welsh's still-fascinating study first appeared nearly thirty years ago; see Welsh, *The Hero of the Waverly Novels* (1963; reprint, New York: Atheneum, 1968). Yet in 1983 Harry E. Shaw could accurately call the Waverley novels "the least-appreciated and least-read body of major fiction in English." Note the adjective "major" in relation to the perceived neglect. See Shaw, *The Forms of Historical Fiction: Sir Walter Scott and His Successors* (Ithaca: Cornell University Press, 1983), 10.

5. Jon Klancher observes that only recently "the rhetorics of English Romantic literature sponsored a criticism that prized imagination, sublimity, and the 'politics of vision'—not because Romantic literature and English politics were felt to be identical, but because they seemed to be so separate." See Klancher, "English Romanticism and Cultural Production," in *The New Historicism*, ed. H. Aram Veeser (New York: Routledge, 1989), 77.

6. See Miriam Allot's collection, *Novelists on the Novel* (London: Routledge and Kegan Paul, 1959), 40–50.

7. Jane Millgate, *Walter Scott: The Making of the Novelist* (Toronto: University of Toronto Press, 1984), vii–ix; Judith Wilt, *Secret Leaves: The Novels of Walter Scott* (Chicago: University of Chicago Press, 1985), 19.

8. David Punter argues that eighteenth-century novelists generally represented the law and its administration from the radical perspective of hostility. See Punter, "Fictional Representation of the Law in the Eighteenth Century," *Eighteenth-Century Studies* 16 (1982): 47–74.

9. William Blackstone, *Commentaries on the Laws of England*, ed. William C. Jones (San Francisco: Bancroft-Whitney, 1916), vol. 2, bk. 4, p. 2165.

10. Toward the end of his career, Scott wrote: "I never could lay down a plan—or having laid it down I never could adhere to it; the action of composition always dilated some passages and abridged or omitted others and personages were rendered important or insignificant not according to their agency in the original conception of the plan but according to the success or otherwise with which I was able to bring them out." See *The Journal of Sir Walter Scott*, ed. W. E. K. Anderson (Oxford: Oxford University Press, 1972), 86, entry for February 12, 1826.

11. Edwin M. Eigner, *The Metaphysical Novel in England and America: Dickens, Bulwer, Melville, and Hawthorne* (Berkeley: University of California Press, 1978), 14–17. Eigner calls attention to the *Journal* passage quoted above.

12. George Levine sees this turn away from realism as a failure of artistic seriousness that occurs throughout the Waverley novels. See Levine, *The Realistic Imagination: English Fiction from Frankenstein to Lady Chatterley* (Chicago: University of Chicago Press, 1981), 85–87.

13. Frederick Burwick draws attention to the king's "benevolent jurisprudence" in his "Scott and Dryden's Ironic Reconciliation," in *Scott and His Influence*, ed. J. H. Alexander and David Hewitt (Aberdeen: Association for Scottish Literature Studies, 1983), 275.

14. Llewellyn Woodward, *The Age of Reform: 1815–1870*, 2d ed. (London: Oxford University Press, 1962), 469–71.

15. Michel Foucault, *Discipline and Punish: The Birth of the Prison*, trans. Alan Sheridan (New York: Pantheon, 1977). For a work focusing on the history of the prison in Great Britain, see Michael Ignatieff, *A Just Measure of Pain: The Penitentiary in the Industrial Revolution, 1750–1850* (New York: Columbia University Press, 1978). John Bender makes literature a part of the complex development of the idea of the prison in *Imagining the Penitentiary: Fiction and the Architecture of Mind in Eighteenth-Century England* (Chicago: University of Chicago Press, 1987).

16. Ignatieff, *A Just Measure of Pain*, 220.

17. Bertrand de Jouvenel, *Power: The Natural History of Its Growth*, trans. J. F. Huntington (London: Batchworth, 1949), 32.

Chapter One: The Lesson of *Waverley*

1. John Locke, *Two Treatises of Government*, 2d ed., ed. Peter Laslett (London: Cambridge University Press, 1970), 286–93, 371.

2. Welsh, *Hero of the Waverley Novels*, 180–83.

3. By dating the composition of the *Two Treatises* well before 1688, not shortly after as had generally been done, Peter Laslett brought into focus fundamental issues concerning Locke's intent; rather than a defense of a completed revolution, the *Two Treatises* becomes a document justifying a coming revolution. Since Laslett's introduction to his edition of the *Two Treatises*, others have made the case for an even more radical Locke on the basis of evidence for a date of composition that refers to specific revolutionary plots. Laslett sees the exclusion crisis as the relevant context. See Laslett's Introduction to Locke, *Two Treatises*, 45–66; Richard Ashcraft, "Revolutionary Politics and Locke's *Two Treatises of Government*: Radicalism and Lockean Political Theory," *Political Theory* 8 (1980): 429–86; George T. Menake, "A Research Note and Query on the Dating of Locke's Two Treatises," *Political Theory* 9 (1981): 547–50.

4. Locke, *Two Treatises*, 299.

5. Welsh identifies Scott's attitude toward the revolution of 1688 with Burke's. Both resist thinking of that event as a precedent. See Welsh, *Hero of the Waverley Novels*, 102.

6. Jeremy Bentham, *Leading Principles of a Constitutional Code*, in *The Works of Jeremy Bentham*, ed. John Bowring (Edinburgh: William Tait, 1843), 9:123.

7. Walter Scott, *Waverley; or, 'Tis Sixty Years Since*, ed. Claire Lamont (Oxford: Clarendon, 1981). All references to *Waverley* are from Lamont's edition and appear in the text. For convenient reference to other editions I cite chapter as well as page numbers.

8. J. M. Beattie notes that in the eighteenth century, the accused was often placed in an extraordinarily weak position: the burden of proof was not carried by the prosecution. See Beattie, *Crime and the Courts in England: 1660–1800* (Princeton: Princeton University Press, 1986), 349.

9. Blackstone, *Commentaries*, vol. 2, bk. 4, pp. 2148–49. The complexity that Blackstone observes in the rules and processes of law lead a modern American legal thinker to argue against the death penalty, for such unavoidable complexity makes errors and arbitrariness inevitable in administering the most absolute of punishments. See Charles L. Black, Jr.,

Capital Punishment: The Inevitability of Caprice and Mistake (New York: Norton, 1974), 14–22.

10. *Sir Walter Scott on Novelists and Fiction*, ed. Ioan Williams (New York: Barnes and Noble, 1968), 193.

11. Robert Kiely maintains that Scott uses Mr. Morton to relieve Waverley of the responsibility for his rebellion. But for my purpose it is important to note that Talbot rescues Waverley from responsibility, rather than relieving him of it. The distinction helps keep Scott's political sympathies more clear than Kiely's argument allows. Still, Kiely is right to note the "political ambiguity" implicit in Scott's subject matter. See Kiely, *The Romantic Novel in England* (Cambridge, Mass.: Harvard University Press, 1972), 147–150. A hypersensitive contemporary reviewer notes this vaguely threatening aspect of *Waverley* in language suggesting that some feelings, principles, or politics are best left unnamed: "it must be observed, that the writer takes upon himself a task of peculiar delicacy, and is attended with peculiar difficulty. For though the period is too remote for prejudices to operate, or animosity to survive, with any degree of formidable strength . . . there are certain feelings still alive, and a certain vigilance still awake, which render the avowal of a partiality for certain principles, and certain politics, though not unsafe, at least unpleasant and invidious." See Anon., review of *Waverley*, *Antijacobin Review* 47 (1814): 218.

12. Kenneth M. Sroka argues that the reader learns from the complementary strengths of Morton and Melville. I agree, but would add that the reader and Scott learn more from Talbot as a concrete embodiment of those strengths. See Sroka, "Education in Walter Scott's *Waverley*," *Studies in Scottish Literature* 15 (1980): 159–60.

13. Locke, *Two Treatises*, 393.

14. Walter Scott, "History of Europe, 1815," *Edinburgh Annual Register* 8, pt. 1 (1817): 314.

15. For a reading that maintains a strong separation between Scott and Talbot, see Jana Davis, "Sir Walter Scott and Enlightenment Theories of the Imagination: *Waverley* and *Quentin Durward*," *Nineteenth-Century Literature* 43 (1989): 454–55.

16. Peter Linebaugh provides a study of attempts (in mid–eighteenth-century England) to increase the terror of execution by making the bodies of victims subject to public dissection. These attempts did not serve the interests of order: crowds allowed the executions, but responded violently against the men hired to carry the bodies away for the surgeons. Scott's own characteristically mixed attitude regarding matters of policy and justice can be noted in his response to the fate of Napoléon. In 1814, Scott wrote that Napoléon's continued life provided the "strongest proof" of the "liberality" of the age. But a year later, after Napoléon's return from Elba

and defeat at Waterloo, he displayed impatience with that liberality: "I believe I shall give offence to my old friends the Whigs by not condoling with Bonaparte. Since his sentence of transportation he has begun to look wonderfully comely in their eyes. I would they hanged him that he might have died a perfect Adonis." See Linebaugh, "The Tyburn Riot Against the Surgeons," in *Albion's Fatal Tree: Crime and Society in Eighteenth-Century England*, by Douglas Hay et al. (New York: Pantheon, 1975), 65–199; *The Letters of Sir Walter Scott*, ed. H. J. C. Grierson (London: Constable, 1932–37), 3:451, 4:100.

17. Scott, "History of Europe, 1815," 314.

18. Asa Briggs sees Sir James Mackintosh's successful motion in 1819 for appointment of a committee of inquiry into the criminal laws as the turning point in reform efforts. See Briggs, *The Age of Improvement: 1783–1867* (London: Longmans, 1959), 217. For an extensive summary of the campaign for reform, see Radzinowicz, *A History of English Criminal Law* 1:497–610.

19. Locke, *Two Treatises*, 292.

20. Francis Hutcheson, *System of Moral Philosophy*, as quoted in James Heath, *Eighteenth-Century Penal Theory* (London: Oxford University Press, 1963), 84.

21. Adam Ferguson, *Institutes of Moral Philosophy* (Mentz: Kupferberg, 1815), 184.

22. Blackstone, *Commentaries*, vol. 2, bk. 4, pp. 2165–66.

23. For a discussion of Bentham's intellectual debt to Beccaria, see H. L. A. Hart, "Bentham and Beccaria," in his *Essays on Bentham: Studies in Jurisprudence and Political Theory* (Oxford: Clarendon, 1982), 40–52.

24. *The Cheap Magazine* 1 (1813), see title page.

25. Martin Madan, *Thoughts on Executive Justice, with Respect to Our Criminal Laws* (London: J. Dodsley, 1785), 11.

26. Ibid., appendix, 54.

27. Ibid., 7.

28. William Paley, *Moral and Political Philosophy*, in *The Works of William Paley* (Edinburgh: Thomas Nelson and Peter Brown, 1831), 13.

29. Such evidence as Paley offers leads Douglas Hay to argue that the criminal law provided the principal means of sustaining the existing social order. Hay follows a similar though even more radical argument developed by Michel Foucault. Foucault insists that the eighteenth-century power structure did not attempt merely to sustain itself. The reform movement becomes for him an especially subtle and successful part of this conspiracy of power. It sought a new " 'economy' of the power to punish," a broader basis for the effective application of power "down to the finest grain of the social body." G. R. Elton warns against such interpretations of historical

evidence, which read intentions in effects. See Douglas Hay, "Property, Authority, and the Criminal Law," in *Albion's Fatal Tree: Crime and Society in Eighteenth-Century England*, by Douglas Hay et al. (New York: Pantheon, 1975), 17–63; Foucault, *Discipline and Punish*, 80; and G. R. Elton, "Crime and the Historian," in *Crime in England: 1550–1800*, ed. J. S. Cockburn (Princeton: Princeton University Press, 1977), 1–14.

30. Paley, *Moral and Political Philosophy*, 131.

31. Ibid., 138.

32. Many of the essays in Gertrude Ezorsky's collection, *Philosophical Perspectives on Punishment* (Albany: State University of New York Press, 1972), take up this issue of guilt's necessary relationship to just punishment. See especially those articles by A. M. Quinton, H. H. McCloskey, and T. L. S. Sprigge.

33. For an interesting and convincing discussion of Scott's perhaps surprising kinship to Bentham on Scottish law reform, see Graham McMaster, *Scott and Society* (Cambridge: Cambridge University Press, 1981), 84–88.

34. Jeremy Bentham, *Principles of Penal Law*, in his *Works* 1:396–98, 404.

35. Romilly's first work on the criminal law, *Observations on a Late Publication Intituled Thoughts on Executive Justice*, was published in 1786, a year after the work by Madan to which it was a direct response.

36. *Memoirs of the Life of Sir Samuel Romilly*, 2d ed., 2 vols. (London: John Murray, 1840) 2:332–33.

37. Anon., article on the *Report of the Select Committee on Criminal Laws: Ordered by the House of Commons to Be Printed, July 19, 1819*, *Edinburgh Review* 35 (1821): 327.

38. Romilly, quoted in anon., review of Samuel Romilly's *Observations on the Criminal Law of England, as It Relates to Capital Punishment*, *Edinburgh Review* 19 (1812): 398.

39. [Robert Southey and John Rickman], "On the Means of Improving the People," *Quarterly Review* 19 (1818): 116.

40. Romilly, *Memoirs* 2:333–38.

41. Dugald Stewart, quoted in ibid., 322, 310n.

42. Scott (like many who sought reform of the criminal law) was more concerned with the apparent cruelty of arbitrary executions than he was with executions themselves. To alleviate overcrowding in prisons, he thought a "great deal . . . might be done by executing the punishment of *death* without a chance of escape in all cases which it should be found properly applicable, of course these occasions being diminished to one out of twenty to which capital punishment is now assigned." See Scott, *Journal*, 430, entry for February 20, 1828.

43. Walter Scott, review article in *Blackwood's Edinburgh Magazine* 2 (1818): 414.

44. Walter Scott, *Demonology and Witchcraft: Letters to J. G. Lockhart, Esq.* (New York: Bell, 1970), 189–90.

45. Ernst Cassirer, *The Myth of the State* (New Haven: Yale University Press, 1946), 146.

46. Scott, *Letters* 3:478.

47. George Levine argues that Waverley's easy acceptance of history's reward sets the context for the novel's punishment scenes. The hero's disengagement emphasizes the reality of historical progress. By this means Scott allows us to sympathize with Fergus and Evan and at the same time makes us understand the need for their destruction. Levine's reading runs counter to those who like myself cannot subordinate the passion of the trial and execution scenes to the "sigh" that signals Waverley's repudiation of romance in favor of "real history." See Levine, *The Realistic Imagination*, 103–6.

Chapter Two: *Old Mortality* and the Right to Punish

1. Francis R. Hart discusses the relevance of the visible expression of legal power to Scott's novels in his "Scott's Endings: The Fictions of Authority," *Nineteenth-Century Fiction* 33 (1978): 48–51.

2. John P. Farrell, *Revolution as Tragedy: The Dilemma of the Moderate from Scott to Arnold* (Ithaca: Cornell University Press, 1980), 92–93, 97–98.

3. David Hewitt, "Scott's Art and Politics," in *Sir Walter Scott: The Long-Forgotten Melody*, ed. Alan Bold (London: Vision, 1983), 43–64.

4. McMaster, *Scott and Society*, 100, 127, et passim. This informative book provides a detailed commentary on Scott's attitudes toward various social and political issues of his day; however, McMaster's persistent denial of history as a theme or subject in the Waverley novels arises from a fairly narrow sense of historiography. Surely *Old Mortality* tells us much about 1817, but that alone does not make it different from any history written in 1817. In any case, *Old Mortality* is conspicuously slighted in McMaster's argument.

5. For useful critical discussions of Scott's relationship to the Scottish school of "philosophical" or "speculative" historians, see Duncan Forbes, "The Rationalism of Sir Walter Scott," *Cambridge Journal* 7 (1953): 20–35; Avrom Fleishman, *The English Historical Novel: Walter Scott to Virginia Woolf* (Baltimore: Johns Hopkins Press, 1971), 37–101; and P. D. Garside, "Scott and the 'Philosophical' Historians," *Journal of the History of Ideas* 36 (1975): 497–512.

6. H. L. A. Hart, *The Concept of Law* (London: Oxford University Press, 1961), 184–95.

7. Jouvenal, *Power*, 37–42.

8. Godfrey Davis, *The Early Stuarts: 1603–1660*, 2d ed. (London: Oxford University Press, 1959), 32–33.

9. Leonard Krieger, *The Politics of Discretion: Pufendorf and the Acceptance of Natural Law* (Chicago: University of Chicago Press, 1965), 11, 80–87, 105; and John M. Wallace, *Destiny His Choice: The Loyalism of Andrew Marvell* (Cambridge: Cambridge University Press, 1968), 34–35.

10. Thomas Hobbes, *Leviathan* (London: Dent, 1973), 166.

11. It is, perhaps, odd to make Monmouth a mouthpiece for Hobbes's doctrine, but his personal mildness and indecisiveness subject him to those, like Claverhouse and Dalzell, who possess stronger and more severe characters. Scott's use of Monmouth in this way serves to diminish the royalist position, just as Dryden's use of Monmouth's malleability in *Absalom and Achitophel* serves to diminish the democratic claims of Shaftesbury. See Scott's *Life of John Dryden* (Lincoln: University of Nebraska Press, 1963), 209.

12. Locke, *Two Treatises*, 297.

13. Ibid., 324.

14. Wilt, *Secret Leaves*, 99.

15. George Goodin sees Morton's appreciation of the limits of politics as the typical wisdom of the political novel: political problems elicit moral responses. But Goodin does not properly credit the very definite political effect Morton has on the action of *Old Mortality*. However uneasily, Morton translates (and compromises) his moral beliefs into political commitment. He does play a role in the uprising of 1679—which in turn anticipates the revolution of 1688. John P. Farrell allows for a more complicated interchange of personal and political values. See Goodin, "Walter Scott and the Tradition of the Political Novel," in *The English Novel in the Nineteenth Century: Essays on the Literary Mediation of Human Values*, ed. George Goodin (Urbana: University of Illinois Press, 1972), 14–24; and Farrell, *Revolution as Tragedy*, 87–100.

16. Locke, *Two Treatises*, 420.

17. Ibid., 209–10.

18. Alexander Welsh, introduction to *Old Mortality*, by Walter Scott (Boston: Houghton Mifflin, 1966), ix–x.

19. Adam Ferguson, *An Essay on the History of Civil Society*, ed. Duncan Forbes (Edinburgh: Edinburgh University Press, 1966), 122.

20. Burke holds that a person in civil society "inclusively, in a great measure, abandons the right of self-defense, the first law of nature." See Edmund Burke, *Reflections on the Revolution in France*, ed. Thomas

H. D. Mahoney (Indianapolis: Bobbs-Merrill, 1955), 68. Peter J. Stanlis, a modern conservative writer on Burke, argues that there is more than a question of emphasis involved in such distinctions as I suggest between Locke and Burke. Stanlis sees Burke as a defender of natural law and civilization against such individualistic writers as Hobbes and Locke. I have used Locke more extensively than Burke in defining Morton's position, but I do not think this use of Locke entirely excludes Burke. The choice is not either/or as Stanlis demands. See Peter J. Stanlis, *Edmund Burke and the Natural Law* (Ann Arbor: University of Michigan Press, 1958), 128–29.

21. Welsh, introduction to *Old Mortality*, x–xiii.

22. Francis R. Hart, *Scott's Novels: The Plotting of Historic Survival* (Charlottesville: University Press of Virginia, 1966), 74-75.

23. Burke, *Reflections*, 197.

24. David Brown, *Walter Scott and the Historical Imagination* (London: Routledge and Kegan Paul, 1979), 83, argues that Morton's political position is historically realistic: "men like Morton, who anticipated the compromise settlement of 1688, certainly existed in Scotland ten years previously." No doubt Brown is right, but I do not believe Scott gives us much reason to believe Morton consciously anticipates the revolution. That understanding belongs to Scott himself, not his character.

25. Ferguson, *Essay*, 20.

26. In his essay on Scott's endings Francis Hart asks, "Was authority ever more than a credible spectacle, a fiction of imagination?" (68). Such pretense does constitute a large measure of authority in the Waverley novels, but it is not the authority Morton seeks. Hart's chapter on *Old Mortality* in *Scott's Novels* offers a fairly positive answer to his own question. Also see Daniel Cottom, *The Civilized Imagination: A Study of Ann Radcliffe, Jane Austen, and Sir Walter Scott* (Cambridge: Cambridge University Press, 1985). Cottom maintains that the pretense of the law reduces the potential of human relationships; violence realizes that potential. But in *Old Mortality* at least, it seems that the false show of the law increases violence with no gain of intimacy.

27. Daniel Whitmore sees both Burley and Claverhouse as adherents of a "literalist mode of interpretation"—a spirit that quite literally kills. See Whitmore, "Bibliolatry and the Rule of the Word: A Study of Scott's *Old Mortality*," *Philological Quarterly* 65 (1986): 244.

28. Ferguson, *Essay*, 63.

29. J. L. Adolphus, *Scott: The Critical Heritage*, ed. John O. Hayden (New York: Barnes and Noble, 1970), 212. Adolphus notes a similar problem with Waverley, who "sinks into absolute insignificance, by sustaining only the part of a common spectator in the highly tragic scene of Mac-

Ivor's and Evan Dhu's condemnation" (213). Adolphus's study, which discusses the works and their authorship, was first published anonymously as *Letters to Richard Heber, Esq. M. P.*, 1821.

30. Gilbert Stuart, *Observations Concerning the Public Law, and the Constitutional History of Scotland: With Occasional Remarks Concerning English Antiquity* (Edinburgh: William Creach, 1779), 278–79.

31. Stuart notes that in "rude times" the severed head of an enemy was used as a conspicuous sign of the victor's power (ibid., 244n–45n). In his Introduction to *A Legend of Montrose* Scott recounts the use of such a sign by a primitive, Highland tribe (140–41). Foucault calls attention to the two-sidedness of such expressions of power in the less rude times of the eighteenth century; see *Discipline and Punish*, 67–69.

32. Paley, *Moral and Political Philosophy*, 137.

33. Daines Barrington, a legal historian and mild reformer, notes with great pride that torture is rare in English history—especially as compared to the histories of other countries of Europe. Barrington adds that "the act of union hath forbid the use of it in Scotland." He is especially sanguine on the progress of the law "upon the most solid and rational principles" since the revolution. See his *Observations on the Statutes, Chiefly the More Ancient, from Magna Charta to the Twenty-first of James the First, Ch. xxvii. with an Appendix; Being a Proposal for New Modelling the Statutes* (London: W. Bowyer, 1766), 56–57, 292, 337.

34. Ferguson, *Essay*, 91.

35. F. R. Hart, "Scott's Endings," 58.

Chapter Three: *Rob Roy* and the Business of Revenge

1. Donald Davie judges *Rob Roy* to be either "a romance spoiled by a cumbrous initial development *or* . . . a realistic novel spoiled by a second half which turns out to be romance." See Davie, *The Heyday of Sir Walter Scott* (New York: Barnes and Noble, 1961), 58.

2. Michael McKeon, *The Origins of the English Novel: 1600–1740* (Baltimore: Johns Hopkins University Press, 1987), 10.

3. Ibid., 21.

4. Wilt, *Secret Leaves*, 8, 69.

5. Cottom, *Civilized Imagination*, 171–72.

6. Ferguson, *Essay*, 217–19.

7. Hobbes, *Leviathan*, 166.

8. Scott's lengthy and informed "Essay on the Drama" was first published in the supplement to the *Encyclopaedia Britannica* (1819). See the reprint in *The Miscellaneous Works of Sir Walter Scott* (Edinburgh: Adam

and Charles Black, 1881), 6:219–395.

9. Hobbes, *Leviathan*, 79.

10. G. W. F. Hegel, *Philosophy of Right*, trans. T. M. Knox (London: Oxford University Press, 1942), 73.

11. Brown, *Scott and the Historical Imagination*, 104.

12. Ibid.

13. Millgate, *Walter Scott*, vii–ix.

14. Jarvie's speech exemplifies the mixture of styles that Alexander Welsh discusses in "Contrast of Styles in the Waverley Novels," *Novel* 6 (1973): 218–28. The dialect has the effect of framing and deflating the high tone of Jarvie's stand.

15. Scott's own rational, as opposed to emotional, loyalty is indicated in a letter written in 1813: "Seriously I am very glad I did not live in 1745 for though as a lawyer I could not have pleaded Charles's right and as a clergyman I could not have prayed for him yet as a soldier I would I am sure against the conviction of my better reason have fought for him even to the bottom of the gallows. But I am not the least afraid nowadays of making my feelings walk hand in hand with my judgement though the former are Jacobitical the latter inclined for public weal to the present succession." *Letters* 3:302.

16. Ferguson, *Essay*, 19, 161–62.

17. Garside, "Scott and the 'Philosophical' Historians," 508.

18. [Francis Jeffrey], review of Mrs. Grant's *Essays on the Superstitions of the Highlanders*, *Edinburgh Review* 18 (1811): 486.

19. Maximillian E. Novak points out that in Defoe's fiction the necessities of survival morally sanction crimes, but at the same time those crimes necessitate laws to punish criminals. The natural law, in short, poses a threat to the established social order. See Novak, *Defoe and the Nature of Man* (London: Oxford University Press, 1963), 65–88.

20. [Jeffrey], review of Mrs. Grant's *Essays*, 487.

21. Ibid., 484.

22. Alexander Welsh treats Frank as a typical Waverley hero burdened by an atypical and tangential moral: Frank, after all, reflects regretfully on his failure to join his father in business. But in the final analysis, Frank's business responsibilities disappear; his right to property is affirmed "morally . . . legally . . . and magically, in the fine recompense of fiction, when Rob Roy slays Rashleigh." See Welsh, *Hero of the Waverley Novels*, 184–86.

23. Richard H. Weisberg, *The Failure of the Word: The Protagonist as Lawyer in Modern Fiction* (New Haven: Yale University Press, 1984), 24–28.

24. Hobbes sharpens his sense of the unending nature of revenge by a perceptive psychological insight that makes even Rashleigh's melodra-

matic fuming somewhat explicable: "To have done more hurt to a man, than he can, or is willing to expiate, enclineth the doer to hate the sufferer. For he must expect revenge, or forgiveness; both which are hatefull" (*Leviathan*, 51). Poor Rashleigh must undergo the pains of revenge *and* forgiveness in the final chapter of *Rob Roy*.

25. Welsh, *Hero of the Waverley Novels*, 187–89.

26. Scott, *Letters* 4:269.

27. Ibid., 436–37, 499, 507–8, et passim. Also see Edgar Johnson, *Sir Walter Scott: The Great Unknown* (New York: Macmillan, 1970), 1:566–71.

28. Millgate, *Walter Scott*, 86.

29. Scott, *Letters* 1:522.

30. Ibid., 521.

Chapter Four: The Frustrations of Justice in *The Heart of Midlothian*

1. Gilbert Stuart, *A View of Society in Europe, in Its Progress from Rudeness to Refinement: Or Inquires Concerning the History of Law, Government, and Manners* (Edinburgh: John Bell, 1778), 39–40.

2. James Dalrymple, Viscount of Stair, *The Institutions of the Law of Scotland*, ed. David M. Walker (Edinburgh: University Press of Edinburgh, 1981), 170.

3. Francis Bacon, "On Revenge," in his *Essays, Advancement of Learning, New Atlantis, and Other Pieces*, ed. Richard Foster Jones (New York: Odyssey, 1937), 17.

4. For a succinct—indeed blunt—assertion of retributive principles, see F. H. Bradley, "The Vulgar Notion of Responsibility in Connexion with the Theories of Free-Will and Necessity," in his *Ethical Studies*, 2d ed. (London: Oxford University Press, 1927), 26–29. Herbert Morris distances retribution from revenge by arguing that the criminal has a "right to punishment," which "derives from a right to be treated as a person." See Morris, "Persons and Punishment," *Monist* 52 (1968): 475–77.

5. Immanuel Kant, *The Metaphysical Elements of Justice*, trans. John Ladd (Indianapolis: Bobbs-Merrill, 1965), 102.

6. Hegel, *Philosophy of Right*, 73.

7. Harry Shaw responds effectively to the common dissatisfaction with Scott that grows from a misunderstanding of his heroine. See Shaw, *Forms of Historical Fiction*, 230.

8. Dorothy Van Ghent, *The English Novel: Form and Function* (New York: Rinehart, 1953), 121.

9. Frances Clements, "'Queens Love Revenge as Well as Their Subjects': Thematic Unity in *The Heart of Midlothian*," *Studies in Scottish*

Literature 10 (1972): 10–17.

10. Fleishman, *English Historical Novel*, 82.

11. A. O. J. Cockshut, *The Achievement of Walter Scott* (New York: New York University Press, 1969), 182.

12. Robin Mayhead, *"The Heart of Midlothian*: Scott as Artist," *Essays in Criticism* 6 (1956): 269. Mayhead sees the prefatory matter as well suited to the thematic concern of the first half of the novel.

13. The description is a curious mixture of Burkean darkness and terror with a matter-of-fact reflection on the salutary qualities of an execution as spectacle. Burke considered a public execution to be a particularly good example of the sublime; see his *On the Sublime and Beautiful*, ed. Charles W. Eliot (New York: Collier, 1909), 43. Burke's essay was first published in 1751. It is surprising that Scott, given his familiarity with eighteenth-century literature, does not tacitly assume the superior utilitarian value of less dramatic modern stagings of execution. Many earlier accounts emphasize the inappropriateness of the festival atmosphere that surrounded the condemned man on his way to death. For example, in Gay's *The Beggar's Opera* (1728) the heroine, Polly, almost hopes her lover, Macheath, will hang, for the pleasure of being the grieving widow of a popular hero nearly equals the pain. Fielding, in his *Inquiry into the Causes of the Late Increase of Robbers* (1751), insisted that executions needed to become more private in order to become more solemn and effective; a criminal should die before a select group of enemies—not a large crowd of friends. See *The Works of Henry Fielding* (London: Heinemann, 1903), 13: 122.

14. For a discussion of the general acceptability of the profession of smuggling, see Cal Winslow, "Sussex Smugglers," in Hay et al., *Albion's Fatal Tree*, 119–66.

15. Bentham allowed for such feelings in his utilitarian analysis. See his *Principles of Penal Law*, 396–98, 404. Of course even those who believe Effie guilty of infanticide or those who hold stern notions of justice would have much sympathy for her. Kant considers infanticide at the hands of the mother a difficult case for legislation to deal with because the crime arises from a sense of honor; therefore, "public legal justice as administered by the state is injustice from the point of view of the people." See Kant, *Metaphysical Elements of Justice*, 106–7.

16. Jean Hampton points out that Hegel's retributive theory is difficult and controversial; Hegel may be taken to argue that the state morally educates criminals by punishing them. Hampton goes on to provide a carefully developed theory of punishment as moral education. See Hampton, "The Moral Education Theory of Punishment," *Philosophy and Public Affairs* 13 (1984): 208–38.

17. Foucault, *Discipline and Punish*, 67–68.

18. David Marshall, *Sir Walter Scott and Scots Law* (Edinburgh: William Hodge, 1932), 126–28.

19. Cesare Beccaria, *On Crimes and Punishments*, trans. Henry Paolucci (Indianapolis: Bobbs-Merrill, 1963), 14–18.

20. Robert C. Gordon notes the intense and complex factionalism that surrounds Porteous and takes the extreme view that the first chapters of the novel "offer a definitive portrait of a world in which Truth is dead— even to the narrator." See Gordon, *Under Which King? A Study of the Scottish Waverley Novels* (Edinburgh: Oliver & Boyd, 1969), 70.

21. Alexander Welsh shows the parallel between the development of the English novel and that of the idea of circumstantial evidence in "Burke and Bentham on the Narrative Potential of Circumstantial Evidence," *New Literary History* 21 (1989–90): 607–27. The layers of authority of authorship that Scott deploys also suggests considerable sophistication on his part regarding the transmission of evidence or of stories. In his own way, Scott seems to raise questions that concern many current theorists prompted by such works as Michel Foucault's "What Is an Author?" in *Language, Counter-Memory, Practice*, ed. Donald F. Bouchard, trans. Bouchard and Sherry Simon (Ithaca: Cornell University Press, 1977), 113–38.

22. Before she considered interfering in Porteous's behalf, Queen Caroline would have done well to note Machiavelli's recounting of Cesare Borgia's astute desertion of an unpopular underling: "[Borgia] named Messer Remirro de Orco, a cruel and vigorous man, to whom he gave absolute powers. In short order this man pacified and unified the whole district, winning thereby great renown. But then the duke decided such excessive authority was no longer necessary, and feared it might become odious; so he set up a civil court in the middle of the province, with an excellent judge and a representative from each city. And because he knew that the recent harshness had generated some hatred, in order to clear the minds of the people and gain them over to his cause completely, he determined to make plain that whatever cruelty had occurred had come, not from him, but from the brutal character of the minister. Taking a proper occasion, therefore, he had him placed on the public square of Cesena one morning, in two pieces, with a piece of wood beside him and a bloody knife. The ferocity of this scene left the people at once stunned and satisfied." See Machiavelli, *The Prince*, trans. Robert M. Adams (New York: Norton, 1977), 22.

23. David Brown is frustrated by the novel's uncertain moral and emotional perspective on the riot that follows Wilson's hanging and the murder of Porteous. Brown's point that Scott slightly muddles these scenes is based upon the implicit assumption that the crowd's action is just. I do not

believe that Scott would grant that assumption. See Brown, *Scott and the Historical Imagination*, 113–15.

24. Georg Lukács, *The Historical Novel*, trans. Hannah and Stanley Mitchell (Lincoln: University of Nebraska Press, 1983), 52.

25. Farrell, *Revolution as Tragedy*, 111.

26. Ibid., 104–5.

27. Welsh, *Hero of the Waverley Novels*, 139.

28. *The Speeches of the Right Hon. Lord Erskine*, ed. James Ridgway, 3d ed. (London: James Ridgway, 1830), 71.

29. Ibid., 72–73, 109.

30. See Jonathan Swift, "The Last Speech and Dying Words of Ebenezor Elliston, Who Was Executed the Second Day of May, 1722," 37–41 in *Irish Tracts, 1720–1723*, vol. 9 of *The Prose Works of Jonathan Smith*, ed. Herbert Davis (Oxford: Blackwell, 1948); and Fielding's *Inquiry*, 118–21.

31. Radzinowicz summarizes opinions concerning the prerogative in *History of English Criminal Law* 1: 126–37.

32. Blackstone, *Commentaries*, vol. 2, bk. 4, pp. 2642–43.

33. Judith Wilt's analysis of Jeanie's role in securing her sister's pardon reveals the profound limits of the heroine's power in a patriarchal society. See Wilt, *Secret Leaves*, 123–26.

34. H. L. A. Hart, "Prolegomenon to the Principles of Punishment," in his *Punishment and Responsibility: Essays in the Philosophy of Law* (London: Oxford University Press, 1968), 1.

35. Ibid., 3.

36. Ibid., 3–13.

Chapter Five: *Ivanhoe* and *The Talisman* as Romances of Justice

1. Foucault, *Discipline and Punish*, 18–24 et passim. In what can be read as an important qualification of Foucault's emphasis on the "gentleness" of modern punishment, Elaine Scarry forcefully reminds us that today's world continues to find value in torture; human suffering is still (more often than we care to think) translated into an "emblem of the regime's strength." See Scarry, *The Body in Pain: The Making and Unmaking of the World* (Oxford: Oxford University Press, 1985), 56–59.

2. Northrop Frye is most unhappy with the critical tendency to place Scott in the tradition of the realistic novel, whereas Edwin Eigner argues that the only romance tradition Scott belongs to is a "bad tradition." See Frye, *The Secular Scripture: A Study of the Structure of Romance* (Cambridge, Mass.: Harvard University Press, 1976), 5–6; and Eigner, *Robert*

Louis Stevenson and the Romantic Tradition (Princeton: Princeton University Press, 1969), 4–5.

3. John O. Hayden briefly surveys the contemporary response to *Ivanhoe* as romance in his introduction to the volume he edited, *Scott: The Critical Heritage* (New York: Barnes and Noble, 1970), 11–12. Also see James T. Hillhouse, *The Waverley Novels and Their Critics* (Minneapolis: University of Minnesota Press, 1936). Joseph E. Duncan attempted to rehabilitate the reputation of *Ivanhoe* by insisting on its essential realism. In a recent and more sophisticated effort to counter the common wisdom concerning *Ivanhoe*, Marilyn Butler points out that *Ivanhoe* is very much engaged with the political world of 1820. But Scott's many references to contemporary controversies in this novel strike me as incidental rather than central. Butler's remark on the "suffering Scott depicts within a medieval and legitimist society" clarifies our differences. She maintains that Scott's picture of that society can be seen as "almost cynical—a world bonded neither by religious ardour nor by chivalric dedication, but by guile and brute force." See Duncan, "The Anti-Romantic in *Ivanhoe*," *Nineteenth-Century Fiction* 9 (1955): 293–300; and M. Butler, *Romantics, Rebels, and Reactionaries: English Literature and Its Background, 1760–1830* (New York: Oxford University Press, 1982), 149–50.

4. [Francis Jeffrey], review of *Ivanhoe*, *Edinburgh Review* 33 (1820): 8, 53–54.

5. Walter Scott, "Essay on Romance," in *Miscellaneous Works* 6:131.

6. [Walter Scott], review, *Quarterly Review* 16 (1817): 448. This anonymous review by Scott of his own work (primarily *Old Mortality*) is reprinted in abridged form in Hayden's *Critical Heritage*.

7. Mark Twain thought a good case could be made for blaming the American Civil War on Scott. For Twain, absurd ideas of honor and social class ferociously held by Southern whites merely reflected values popularized by "Sir Walter": "It was Sir Walter that made every gentleman in the South a Major or a Colonel, or a General or a Judge, before the war; and it was he, also, that made these gentlemen value these bogus decorations. For it was he that created rank and caste down there, and also reverence for rank and caste, and pride and pleasure in them." Significantly, *Ivanhoe* is the only Waverley novel Twain specifically mentions in his attack— and for the most part the only one he seems to have in mind. See Twain's *Life on the Mississippi*, in *Mississippi Writings* (New York: Library of America, 1982), 500–502. Twain's work first appeared in 1883.

8. Walter Bagehot, "The Waverley Novels," in his *Literary Studies* (New York: Dutton, 1950), 2:149.

9. Alice Chandler, "Chivalry and Romance: Scott's Medieval Novels," *Studies in Romanticism* 14 (1975): 197. See also Chandler's *A Dream*

of Order: The Medieval Ideal in Nineteenth-Century English Literature (Lincoln: University of Nebraska Press, 1970), 35–39.

10. P. D. Garside, "Scott, the Romantic Past and the Nineteenth Century," *Review of English Studies*, n.s., 23 (1972): 147–50; Wilt, *Secret Leaves*, 18–48. Garside, who marshals an impressive collection of supporting documents to complicate and question Chandler's reading of Scott's medieval novels, makes an important concession toward the end of his essay: "But the search for 'themes' in the medieval novels can be dangerous. Essentially, they are 'pictures' of a colorful era, with which Scott attempted to revive the jaded appetite of his readers. There can be little doubt that he, himself, was happier in the more realistic vein of the Scottish novels" (156–57).

11. Francis Hart makes much of Saladin's refusal to accept Richard's challenge, but I do not believe that it changes the more general impression established by the rest of the novel. We should remember that this final challenge differs from others I discuss in that it addresses no wrong. Saladin already possesses his proper domain; he does not need to play to Richard's delight in gamesmanship. See F. R. Hart, *Scott's Novels*, 153, 175–180.

12. Foucault, *Discipline and Punish*, 42–47.

13. Fielding, *Causes of the Late Increases of Robbers*, 123; Beccaria, *Crimes and Punishments*, 55–57; Blackstone, *Commentaries*, vol. 2, bk. 4, p. 2650; Bentham, *Principles of Penal Law*, 402.

14. Walter Scott, "Essay on Chivalry," in *Miscellaneous Works* 6:46.

15. Ibid., 49, 85–92, 118–19.

16. Francis Hart considers "humane realism" to be the lesson of the medieval novels. I am not convinced that the attitudes of the most virtuous characters in *The Talisman* are especially humane or realistic even at the novel's end. See F. R. Hart, *Scott's Novels*, 175.

17. Beccaria, *Crimes and Punishments*, 45.

18. William Wordsworth, "Sonnets on Punishment by Death," *Quarterly Review* 69 (1841): 39–49. For perhaps the only sympathetic modern analysis of the sonnets on capital punishment, see Seraphia D. Leyda, "Wordsworth's Sonnets Upon the Punishment of Death," *Wordsworth Circle* 14 (1983): 48–53. Leyda insists that Wordsworth's purpose was not to defend the status quo. Rather, she argues, the sonnets address specific efforts to eliminate capital punishment entirely. Although her point concerning the sonnets seems fair, such an abolitionist movement had long been part of the reform effort; Wordsworth's specific argument may have been an effective strategy in opposing a more general movement. Certainly the commentary by Henry Taylor that accompanies the sonnets in the *Quarterly Review* expresses suspicion concerning even modest reform.

19. James Heath, *Eighteenth-Century Penal Theory* (London: Oxford University Press, 1963), 61. Also see Blackstone, *Commentaries*, vol. 2, bk. 4, p. 2165.

20. Hegel, *Philosophy of Right*, 70–71.

21. Kant, *Metaphysical Elements of Justice*, 104–5.

22. Hobbes, *Leviathan*, 72.

23. For a survey of Jacobin fiction and its formulaic attack on the law, see Marilyn Butler, *Jane Austen and the War of Ideas* (London: Oxford University Press, 1975), 46–75. See also Maximillian E. Novak, *Eighteenth-Century English Literature* (New York: Schocken, 1984), 186–88.

24. Jeremy Bentham, *An Introduction to the Principles of Morals and Legislation*, ed. J. H. Burns and H. L. A. Hart (London: Athlone, 1970), 158.

25. Plato, *Gorgias*, trans. B. Jowett, in *The Dialogues of Plato* (New York: Scribner's, 1911), 3:63–69. Even Bentham uses the crime/sickness, punishment/cure analogy. In Samuel Butler's *Erewhon* (1872) this analogy is subject to an extended, playful variation: Erewhonian "straighteners" or physicians prescribe cures for wrong-doers; Erewhonian courts inflict punishments on the sick. See Bentham, *Works* 1:400; and Samuel Butler, *Erewhon, or, Over the Range* (New York: Random House, 1927), 88–101.

26. Welsh, *Hero of the Waverley Novels*, 63–65.

Chapter Six: Redgauntlet as a Romance of Power

1. Thomas Noon Talfourd, review of *Redgauntlet*, *New Monthly Magazine* 11 (1824): 94.

2. Ibid., 96.

3. John H. Langbein argues convincingly that the "fairy tale" of a progressive, humane spirit does not, in fact, account for the disappearance of torture on the Continent and in Great Britain. Modern historians, he maintains, have been greatly misled by the attention lavished on such reformers as Beccaria by Enlightenment writers. The development of a new system of proof made torture simply unnecessary; it did not appeal so much to humanity as to judicial efficiency. See Langbein, *Torture and the Law of Proof: Europe and England in the Ancien Régime* (Chicago: University of Chicago Press, 1977) 10–12.

4. Ferguson, *Essay*, 240.

5. For a study of the passive hero as a hero of a property-based society, see Welsh, *Hero of the Waverley Novels*.

6. McMaster, *Scott and Society*, 45–47.

7. Jouvenal, *Power*, 33.

8. Blackstone's concessions to the English law's imperfections are often prefaced by elaborate assertions of its essential goodness: "But even with us in England, where our crown law is with justice supposed to be more nearly advanced to perfection; where crimes are more accurately defined and penalties less uncertain and arbitrary; where all our accusations are public and our trials in the face of the world; where torture is unknown, and every delinquent is judged by such of his equals, against whom he can form no exception nor even a personal dislike,—even here we shall occasionally find room to remark some particulars that seem to want revision and amendment." Blackstone, *Commentaries*, vol. 2, bk. 4, p. 2149.

9. M. Butler, *Romantics, Rebels, and Reactionaries*, 111.

10. William Hazlitt, *The Spirit of the Age; or, Contemporary Portraits*, 2d ed. (London: Henry Colburn, 1825), 123–45. Hazlitt's essay was first published in *New Monthly Magazine* 10 (1824): 297–304.

11. Thomas Carlyle, review of Lockhart's *Life of Scott*, *London and Westminster Review* 28 (1838): 293–345.

12. Scott had little confidence that the growing industrial class could accurately identify or effectively act upon their own interests; immediate desires would blind them to lasting benefits. He feared the Whig presumption that the populace could act rationally. In 1825 he wrote: "It takes only the hand of a Liliputian to light a fire but would require the diuretic powers of Gulliver to extinguish it. The Whigs will live and die in the heresy that the world is ruled by little pamphlets and speeches and that if you can sufficiently demonstrate that a line of conduct is most consistent with men's interest you have therefore and thereby demonstrate[d] that they will at length after a few speeches on the subject adopt it of course." See Scott, *Journal*, 12; entry for November 25, 1825.

13. Brown, *Scott and the Historical Imagination*, 171.

14. For an excellent discussion of Scott's complicated attitude toward history and its narrative shaping, see James Kerr, "Fiction Against History: Scott's *Redgauntlet* and the Power of Romance," *Texas Studies in Literature and Language* 29 (1987): 237–60.

15. Beattie, *Crime and the Courts in England*, 421–23.

16. Foucault, *Discipline and Punish*, 24.

17. Ibid., 67–68.

18. Lennard J. Davis sees the tension arising from the contrary moral and political signals inherent in criminal stories as one that "powers the novel's form." Davis is concerned with the eighteenth-century novel, but his argument has relevance to Scott. By writing historical novels, Scott may be seen as attempting to resolve the tension by distancing the critical implications of realistic fiction. See Davis, *Factual Fictions: The Origins of*

the English Novel (New York: Columbia University Press, 1983), 134–37.

19. Judith Wilt argues that thoughts and fears of parricide constitute a central anxiety of the Scott hero. Perhaps in *Redgauntlet* Scott dissolves even that tension. See Wilt, *Secret Leaves*, 42, 128–29.

20. David Daiches, "Scott's *Redgauntlet*," in *From Jane Austen to Joseph Conrad*, ed. Robert C. Rathburn and Martin Steinman, Jr. (Minneapolis: University of Minnesota Press, 1958), 54–56.

21. Cockshut, *Achievement of Scott*, 210.

22. Levine, *Realistic Imagination*, 121.

23. Gordon, *Under Which King?*, 107, 167.

24. Beccaria, *Crimes and Punishments*, 46.

25. Jouvenel, *Power*, 39–42. Jouvenel argues that Locke provides a lame qualification of the explicit authoritarianism of Hobbes by claiming that individuals withhold some rights from the collective power. Such a reservation provides a political escape route, but does not offer a logically consistent position; for who would judge in conflicts arising between those remaining individual rights? The advantages of the social contract disappear when man can claim to be a judge in his own case.

26. F. R. Hart, "Scott's Endings," 50–51.

27. Gordon calls attention to the "Conclusion by Dr. Dryasdust," which breaks the spell of the novel's closing chapter. See Gordon, *Under Which King?*, 166–67.

28. Foucault, *Discipline and Punish*, 106.

29. Kant, *Metaphysical Elements of Justice*, 103–4.

Postscript on the Prison

1. Bender, *Imagining the Penitentiary*; D. A. Miller, *The Novel and the Police* (Berkeley: University of California Press, 1988).

2. Gordon, *Under Which King?*, 28–29.

3. William Godwin, *The Adventures of Caleb Williams, or Things as They Are* (New York: Rinehart, 1960), 210.

4. Mary Wollstonecraft, *Maria, or the Wrongs of Women* (New York: Norton, 1975), 27.

5. Ibid., 52–53.

6. Ibid., 64.

7. Victor Brombert, *The Romantic Prison: The French Tradition* (Princeton: Princeton University Press, 1978), 62–77.

8. Bender, *Imagining the Penitentiary*, 37, 50–51. Bender maintains that even sentences impose a structure that reflects the logic of the penitentiary, but I would argue that a prison sentence moves more slowly and

less purposefully than one of Scott's most elaborate verbal sentences.

9. Miller, *The Novel and the Police*, vii–x.

10. Alexander Welsh turns our attention to the endings of narratives in his review of Bender's *Imagining the Penitentiary, Eighteenth-Century Studies* 21 (1988): 376.

11. Perhaps the sharing of a cell by Nigel and Margaret in *The Fortunes of Nigel* should further prompt us to look at the marriages that end the Waverley novels in context of the prison.

Selected Bibliography

1. Walter Scott: Primary Sources

A Collection of Scarce and Valuable Tracts, on the Most Interesting and Entertaining Subjects: But Chiefly Such as Relate to the History and Constitution of These Kingdoms. 2d. ed. Edited by Walter Scott. 13 vols. London: T. Cadell and W. Davies, 1815.

Demonology and Witchcraft: Letters to J. G. Lockhart, Esq. New York: Bell, 1970.

"History of Europe, 1815." *Edinburgh Annual Register* 8, pt. 1 (1817): 1–373.

The Journal of Sir Walter Scott. Edited by W. E. K. Anderson. Oxford: Oxford University Press, 1972.

The Letters of Sir Walter Scott. 12 vols. Edited by H. J. C. Grierson. London: Constable, 1932–37.

The Life of John Dryden. Lincoln: University of Nebraska Press, 1963.

The Miscellaneous Works of Sir Walter Scott. Vol. 6 (contains the essays on romance, chivalry, and the drama). Edinburgh: Adam and Charles Black, 1881.

Sir Walter Scott on Novelists and Fiction. Edited by Ioan Williams. New York: Barnes and Noble, 1968.

The Waverley Novels. Dryburgh Edition. 25 vols. Edinburgh: Adam and Charles Black, 1893–94.

Waverley, or 'Tis Sixty Years Since. Edited by Claire Lamont. Oxford: Clarendon, 1981.

2. Scott Criticism, Literary History, and Theory

Allot, Miriam. *Novelists on the Novel.* London: Routledge and Kegan Paul, 1959.

Anon. Review of *Waverley. Antijacobin Review* 47 (1814): 217–47.

Bagehot, Walter. "The Waverley Novels." In his *Literary Studies*, vol. 2. New York: Dutton, 1950.

Bender, John. *Imagining the Penitentiary: Fiction and the Architecture of Mind in Eighteenth-Century England*. Chicago: University of Chicago Press, 1987.

Brombert, Victor. *The Romantic Prison: The French Tradition*. Princeton: Princeton University Press, 1978.

Brown, David. *Walter Scott and the Historical Imagination*. London: Routledge and Kegan Paul, 1979.

Burwick, Frederick. "Scott and Dryden's Ironic Reconciliation." In *Scott and His Influence*, edited by J. H. Alexander and David Hewitt. Aberdeen: Association for Scottish Literature Studies, 1983.

Butler, Marilyn. *Jane Austen and the War of Ideas*. London: Oxford University Press, 1975.

————. *Romantics, Rebels, and Reactionaries: English Literature and Its Background, 1760–1830*. New York: Oxford University Press, 1982.

Chandler, Alice. "Chivalry and Romance: Scott's Medieval Novels." *Studies in Romanticism* 14 (1975): 185–200.

————. *A Dream of Order: The Medieval Ideal in Nineteenth-Century English Literature*. Lincoln: University of Nebraska Press, 1970.

Cockshut, A. O. J. *The Achievement of Walter Scott*. New York: New York University Press, 1969.

Cottom, Daniel. *The Civilized Imagination: A Study of Ann Radcliffe, Jane Austen, and Sir Walter Scott*. Cambridge: Cambridge University Press, 1985.

Daiches, David. "Scott's *Redgauntlet*." In *From Jane Austen to Joseph Conrad*, edited by Robert C. Rathburn and Martin Steinman, Jr. Minneapolis: University of Minnesota Press, 46–59.

Davis, Lennard J. *Factual Fictions: The Origins of the English Novel*. New York: Columbia University Press, 1983.

Eigner, Edwin M. *The Metaphysical Novel in England and America: Dickens, Bulwer, Melville, and Hawthorne*. Berkeley: University of California Press, 1978.

————. *Robert Louis Stevenson and the Romantic Tradition*. Princeton: Princeton University Press, 1969.

Farrell, John P. *Revolution as Tragedy: The Dilemma of the Moderate from Scott to Arnold*. Ithaca: Cornell University Press, 1980.

Fleishman, Avrom. *The English Historical Novel: Walter Scott to Virginia Woolf*. Baltimore: Johns Hopkins Press, 1971.

Forbes, Duncan. "The Rationalism of Sir Walter Scott." *Cambridge Journal* 7 (1953): 20–35.

Foucault, Michel. "What Is an Author." In his *Language, Counter-Memory, Practice*, edited by Donald F. Bouchard; translated by Bouchard and Sherry Simon. Ithaca: Cornell University Press, 1977.

Frye, Northrop. *The Secular Scripture: A Study in the Structure of Romance*. Cambridge, Mass.: Harvard University Press, 1976.

Garside, P. D. "Scott and the 'Philosophical' Historians." *Journal of the History of Ideas* 36 (1975): 497–512.

———. "Scott, the Romantic Past and the Nineteenth Century." *Review of English Studies*, n.s., 23 (1972): 147–61.

Goodin, George. "Walter Scott and the Tradition of the Political Novel." In *The English Novel in the Nineteenth Century: Essays on the Literary Mediation of Human Values*, edited by George Goodin. Urbana: University of Illinois Press, 1972.

Gordon, Robert C. *Under Which King? A Study of the Scottish Waverley Novels*. Edinburgh: Oliver and Boyd, 1969.

Hart, Francis R. "Scott's Endings: The Fictions of Authority." *Nineteenth-Century Fiction* 33 (1978): 48–68.

———. *Scott's Novels: The Plotting of Historic Survival*. Charlottesville: University Press of Virginia, 1966.

Hayden, John O., ed. *Scott: The Critical Heritage*. New York: Barnes and Noble, 1970.

Hazlitt, William. *The Spirit of the Age; or, Contemporary Portraits*. 2d ed. London: Henry Colburn, 1825.

Hewitt, David. "Scott's Art and Politics." In *Sir Walter Scott: The Long-Forgotten Melody*, edited by Alan Bold. London: Vision, 1983.

Hillhouse, James T. *The Waverley Novels and Their Critics*. Minneapolis: University of Minnesota Press, 1936.

[Jeffrey, Francis]. Review of *Ivanhoe*. *Edinburgh Review* 33 (1820): 1–54.

Johnson, Edgar. *Sir Walter Scott: The Great Unknown*. 2 vols. New York: Macmillan, 1970.

Kerr, James. "Fiction Against History: Scott's *Redgauntlet* and the Power of Romance." *Texas Studies in Literature and Language* 29 (1987): 237–60.

Klancher, Jon. "English Romanticism and Cultural Production." In *The New Historicism*, edited by H. Aram Veeser. New York: Routledge, 1989.

Levine, George. *The Realistic Imagination: English Fiction from Frankenstein to Lady Chatterley*. Chicago: University of Chicago Press, 1981.

Lukács, Georg. *The Historical Novel*. Translated by Hannah and Stanley Mitchell. Lincoln: University of Nebraska Press, 1983.

McKeon, Michael. *The Origins of the English Novel: 1660–1740*. Baltimore: Johns Hopkins University Press, 1987.

McMaster, Graham. *Scott and Society*. Cambridge: Cambridge University Press, 1981.

Miller, D. A. *The Novel and the Police*. Berkeley: University of California Press, 1988.

Millgate, Jane. *Walter Scott: The Making of a Novelist*. Toronto: University of Toronto Press, 1984.

Novak, Maximillian E. *Defoe and the Nature of Man*. London: Oxford University Press, 1963.

Punter, David. "Fictional Representation of the Law in the Eighteenth Century." *Eighteenth-Century Studies* 16 (1982): 47–74.

Shaw, Harry E. *The Forms of Historical Fiction: Sir Walter Scott and His Successors*. Ithaca: Cornell University Press, 1983.

[Talfourd, Thomas Noon]. Review of *Redgauntlet*. *New Monthly Magazine* 11 (1824): 93–96.

Van Ghent, Dorothy. *The English Novel: Form and Function*. New York: Rinehart, 1953.

Weisberg, Richard H. *The Failure of the Word: The Protagonist as Lawyer in Modern Fiction*. New Haven: Yale University Press, 1984.

Welsh, Alexander. "Burke and Bentham on the Narrative Potential of Circumstantial Evidence." *New Literary History* 21 (1989–90): 607–27.

———. *The Hero of the Waverley Novels*. 1963. Reprint. New York: Atheneum, 1968.

———. Introduction to *Old Mortality*, by Walter Scott. Boston: Houghton Mifflin, 1966.

Whitmore, Daniel. "Bibliolatry and the Rule of the Word: A Study of Scott's *Old Mortality*." *Philological Quarterly* 65 (1986): 244.

Wilt, Judith. *Secret Leaves: The Novels of Walter Scott*. Chicago: University of Chicago Press, 1985.

3. Punishment: The Legal, Philosophical, and Historical Context

Anon. Article on the *Report of the Select Committee on Criminal Laws: Ordered by the House of Commons to Be Printed, July 19, 1819*. *Edinburgh Review* 35 (1821): 314–53.

Anon. Review of Samuel Romilly's *Observations on the Criminal Law of England, as It Relates to Capital Punishment*. *Edinburgh Review* 19 (1812): 389–415.

Ashcraft, Richard. "Revolutionary Politics and Locke's *Two Treatises of Government*: Radicalism and Lockean Political Theory." *Political Theory* 8 (1980): 429–86.

Bacon, Francis. "On Revenge." In his *Essays, Advancement of Learning, New Atlantis, and Other Pieces*. Edited by Richard Foster Jones. New York: Odyssey, 1937.

Barrington, Daines. *Observations on the Statutes, Chiefly the More Ancient, from Magna Charta to the Twenty-first of James the First, Ch. xxvii. with an Appendix; Being a Proposal for New Modelling the Stat-*

utes. London: W. Bowyer, 1766.

Beattie, J. M. *Crime and the Courts in England: 1660–1800.* Princeton: Princeton University Press, 1986.

Beccaria, Cesare. *On Crimes and Punishments.* Translated by Henry Paolucci. Indianapolis: Bobbs-Merrill, 1963.

Bentham, Jeremy. *An Introduction to the Principles of Morals and Legislation.* Edited by J. H. Burns and H. L. A. Hart. London: Athlone, 1970.
———. *Principles of Penal Law.* In vol. 1 of *The Works of Jeremy Bentham,* edited by John Bowring. Edinburgh: William Tait, 1843.

Berns, Walter. *For Capital Punishment: Crime and the Morality of the Death Penalty.* New York: Basic Books, 1979.

Black, Charles L., Jr. *Capital Punishment: The Inevitability of Caprice and Mistake.* New York: Norton, 1974.

Blackstone, William. *Commentaries on the Laws of England.* Edited by William C. Jones. 2 vols. San Francisco: Bancroft-Whitney, 1916.

Briggs, Asa. *The Age of Improvement: 1783–1867.* London: Longmans, 1959.

Bradley, F. H. "The Vulgar Notion of Responsibility in Connexion with the Theories of Free-Will and Necessity." In his *Ethical Studies,* 2d ed. London: Oxford University Press, 1927.

Burke, Edmund. *On the Sublime and Beautiful.* Edited by Charles W. Eliot. New York: Collier, 1909.
———. *Reflections on the Revolution in France.* Edited by Thomas H. D. Mahoney. Indianapolis: Bobbs-Merrill, 1955.

Elton, G. R. "Crime and the Historian." In *Crime in England: 1550–1800,* edited by J. S. Cockburn. Princeton: Princeton University Press, 1977.

Erskine, William. *The Speeches of the Right Hon. Lord Erskine.* 3d ed. Edited by James Ridgway. London: James Ridgway, 1830.

Ezorsky, Gertrude, ed. *Philosophical Perspectives on Punishment.* Albany: State University of New York Press, 1972.

Ferguson, Adam. *An Essay on the History of Civil Society.* Edited by Duncan Forbes. Edinburgh: Edinburgh University Press, 1966.
———. *Institutes of Moral Philosophy.* Mentz: Kupferberg, 1815.

Fielding, Henry. *Inquiry into the Causes of the Late Increase of Robbers.* In vol. 13 of *The Works of Henry Fielding.* London: Heinemann, 1903.

Foucault, Michel. *Discipline and Punish: The Birth of the Prison.* Translated by Alan Sheridan. New York: Pantheon, 1977.

Hampton, Jean. "The Moral Education Theory of Punishment." *Philosophy and Public Affairs* 13 (1984): 208–38.

Hart, H. L. A. "Bentham and Beccaria." In his *Essays on Bentham: Studies in Jurisprudence and Political Theory.* Oxford: Clarendon, 1982.
———. *The Concept of Law.* London: Oxford University Press, 1961.

————. "Prolegomenon to the Principles of Punishment." In his *Punishment and Responsibility: Essays in the Philosophy of Law*. London: Oxford University Press, 1968.

Hay, Douglas, et al. *Albion's Fatal Tree: Crime and Society in Eighteenth-Century England*. New York: Pantheon, 1975.

Heath, James. *Eighteenth-Century Penal Theory*. London: Oxford University Press, 1963.

Hegel, G. W. F. *Philosophy of Right*. Translated by T. M. Knox. London: Oxford University Press, 1942.

Hobbes, Thomas. *Leviathan*. London: Dent, 1973.

Ignatieff, Michael. *A Just Measure of Pain: The Penitentiary in the Industrial Revolution in England, 1750–1850*. New York: Columbia University Press, 1978.

[Jeffrey, Francis]. Review of Mrs. Grant's *Essays on the Superstitions of the Highlanders*. *Edinburgh Review* 18 (1811): 480–510.

Jouvenel, Bertrand de. *Power: The Natural History of Its Growth*. Translated by J. F. Huntington. London: Batchworth, 1949.

Kant, Immanuel. *The Metaphysical Elements of Justice*. Translated by John Ladd. Indianapolis: Bobbs-Merrill, 1965.

Krieger, Leonard. *The Politics of Discretion: Pufendorf and the Acceptance of Natural Law*. Chicago: University of Chicago Press, 1965.

Langbein, John. *Torture and the Law of Proof: Europe and England in the Ancien Régime*. Chicago: University of Chicago Press, 1977.

Locke, John. *Two Treatises of Government*. 2d ed. Edited by Peter Laslett. London: Cambridge University Press, 1970.

Madan, Martin. *Thoughts on Executive Justice, with Respect to Our Criminal Laws*. London: J. Dodsley, 1785.

Paley, William. *Moral and Political Philosophy*. In *The Works of William Paley*. Edinburgh: Thomas Nelson and Peter Brown, 1831.

Radzinowicz, Leon. *A History of English Criminal Law and Its Administration from 1750*. 4 vols. London: Stevens and Sons, 1948.

Romilly, Samuel. *Memoirs of the Life of Sir Samuel Romilly*. 2d ed. 2 vols. London: John Murray, 1840.

Scarry, Elaine. *The Body in Pain: The Making and Unmaking of the World*. Oxford: Oxford University Press, 1985.

[Southey, Robert, and John Rickman]. "On the Means of Improving the People." *Quarterly Review* 19 (1818): 79–115.

Stuart, Gilbert. *Observations Concerning the Public Law, and the Constitutional History of Scotland: With Occasional Remarks Concerning English Antiquity*. Edinburgh: William Creech, 1779.

Swift, Jonathan. "The Last Speech and Dying Words of Ebenezor Elliston, Who Was Executed the Second Day of May, 1722." In *Irish Tracts*,

1720–1723, vol. 9 of *The Prose Works of Jonathan Swift*, edited by Herbert Davis. Oxford: Blackwell, 1948.

[Taylor, Henry]. Commentary on and introduction to Wordsworth's *Sonnets upon the Punishment of Death*. *Quarterly Review* 69 (1841): 1–52. (Includes first printing of *Sonnets*.)

Wallace, John M. *Destiny His Choice: The Loyalism of Andrew Marvell*. Cambridge: Cambridge University Press, 1968.

Woodward, Llewellyn. *The Age of Reform: 1815–1870*. 2d ed. London: Oxford University Press, 1962.

Index

Miller, David, 118, 120, 121
Millgate, Jane, 4, 52, 60
Moll Flanders, 13, 56
Montesquieu, 100

Natural law, 31–33, 37, 130–31
    (n. 20), 133 (n. 19)

Old Mortality, viii, 7, 8, 10, 27,
    28–44, 45, 66, 83–84, 102

Paley, William, 22–26, 42–43,
    88, 92
Peveril of the Peak, 8–9, 119, 121
Philosophical history, 41–42, 46–
    48, 54–58, 102. *See also*
    Ferguson
Popular culture, xi, 82, 90–91, 94,
    106
Power: defensiveness of, vii;
    responsibilities of, 1–2; basis of,
    32–34, 113–15; and self
    preservation, 92; and passivity,
    102–3; awareness of interests,
    106–7; punishment's role in
    growth of, 114, 127 (n. 29)
Prerogative, 71, 78–80
Prison, x, 9, 118–22, 143 (n. 11)
Punishment: history of, vii, 9–10,
    42, 102; responsibility and right,
    1–2, 38; expressive function of,
    9, 20; as utilitarian act, 12–13,
    21–25, 64, 66, 67–69, 73, 80, 116;
    as retribution, 64–65, 66, 72, 80,
    117, 134 (n. 4), 135 (n. 16);
    proximity to judgment, 86; as
    means of healing, 95, 97–99, 140
    (n. 25); instrumental view of,
    105–6. *See also* Capital
    punishment, Execution, Prison,
    Torture

Quentin Durward, 2–3, 8, 82

Radzinowicz, Leon, 78
Realism. *See* Genre
Redgauntlet, ix, x, 4, 7, 8, 9, 10,
    12, 99, 100–117
Retribution. *See* Punishment
Revenge: revenge tragedy, 48–49,
    59; judge's control of, 62–65;
    distinguished from retribution,
    64–65; Hobbes on, 133–34 (n. 24)
Rickman, John, 25
Rob Roy, viii, 4, 7, 10, 44, 45–61,
    87–88, 98, 100
Romance. *See* Genre
Romilly, Sir Samuel, 11, 22, 25–26

Scott, Walter: in relation to
    surrounding political culture,
    vii–viii, 36, 45, 103–4, 126–27
    (n. 16), 128 (n. 42), 133 (n. 15),
    141 (n. 12); on Revolution of
    1688, 5, 12, 29, 35–36, 41, 102;
    his fame and anonymity, 5, 47,
    60; on economic speculation, 59
Shakespeare, xi–xii, 23
Social contract, 1, 11–12, 32–36,
    87–92, 114, 142 (n. 25)
Southey, Robert, 24
Stair, Lord, 63–64
Stendhal, 121
Stewart, Dugald, 26
Stuart, Gilbert, 41, 62–65, 69, 78
Suicide, 27, 89–90
Swift, Jonathan, 78

Tale of Two Cities, A, 88
Talfourd, Thomas Noon, 100–102,
    103, 111
Talisman, The, 4, 6–7, 8, 81–99,
    107